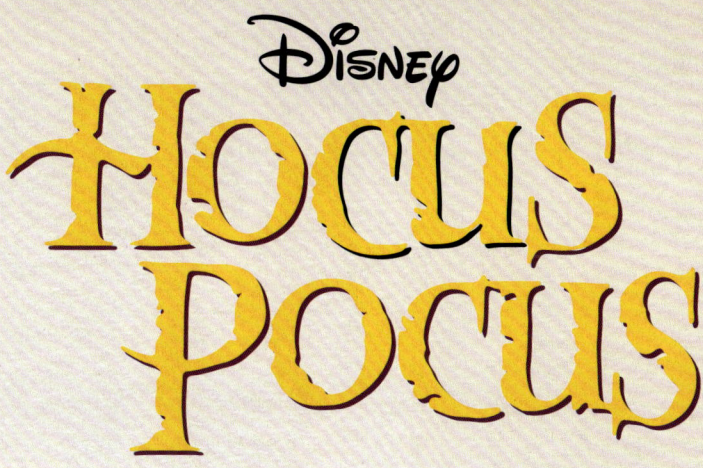

Hocus Pocus

The Official Cookbook

RECIPES INSPIRED BY THE
SANDERSON SISTERS,
MAX, DANI, AND BEYOND

BY ELENA CRAIG & S. T. BENDE

INSIGHT
EDITIONS

SAN RAFAEL • LOS ANGELES • LONDON

Table of Contents

Introduction 7

Appetizers and Sides 9

Billy Butcherson Zombie Fingers 10
All Hallows' Eve Feast Grazing Board 13
Miss Olin Nutty Brown Bread 17
Pretty Black Meatball Spiders 18
"Amok, Amok, Amok" Guacamole and Homemade Chips 21
"No Witches Here" Pumpkin Butter 22
The Master's Fried Peppers 23
Dead Man's Toes 25
"Oh, Cheese and Crust" Homemade Crackers 26
Popping Cranberries 27
Roach Muffins 29
Pastry Boots 30

Main Dishes 33

Mrs. Dennison's Roasted Pumpkin Tacos 35
Shishkebaby 37
Knockout Skillet French Toast 38
Full Moon Blue Cheese Onion Tart 41
Mummy's Scorpion Pie 45
"Who's Going for the Jacuzzi" Lobster 47
Spicy Cauliflower Ears 48
Roasted Red Spice Chicken 49
Maggot-Stuffed Pork Chop 50
Green Mummy Roll Ups 53
Spicy Nightshade Stir-Fry 56
Waterwheel Pot Pie 59
Sanderson Sisters Barbecue Fillet 61
Cheese Puff Chicken Tenders 63
Hollywood Barbecue Chicken Pizza 65
Tie-Dye California Smoothie Bowl 66

Desserts 69

Thackery Binx Treats 70
"Hey, Cupcake" Cupcakes 73
Winnie's Spellbook Cake 77
Classic Caramel Apple Dip 81
Broomstick, and Other Transport, Treats 83
Winnie's Magical Popping Candy 86
Black River Brownie Bars 87
Witch Cookie Pop 89
Dad-cula Fang Strawberries 93
Twisted Winifred Spirals 94
Puffed Rice Potion Bottles 97
Tart Face Tart 98
Cat Tongue Cookies 101
Frog Eggs Boba Matcha Cheesecake 103
Dust Bombs 105

Drinks 107

Most Refreshing Drink 109
"I Put a Spell on You" Brew 110
Life Potion Witches' Drink 113
Pumpkin Spiced Golden Milk 114
Burning Rain of Death Drink 115
Winnie's Popping Potion 117
Sarah's Sassy Sipper 118
Mary's Magic Elixir 121
Sunrise Punch 122

Conclusion 125

Glossary 126

Introduction

The magical world of *Hocus Pocus* has put a spell on us from the moment we first met its charmingly cursed sisters. With their penchant for plotting, fondness for mischief, and unrelenting spirits of determination, Winifred, Mary, and Sarah Sanderson have inspired the curious, the daring, and of course, the adventurous souls ever since they first arrived in Salem. And while some of the sisters' schemes *may* have been slightly unscrupulous, one need not view their plotting through fearful eyes. After all, as they say, the legend of the Sanderson sisters is just a bunch of *hocus pocus*, right?

But even legends have their dangers, dancing—as they so often do—along the razor-thin veil that separates truth and fantasy. After a three-hundred-year absence, the Sandersons are more than ready to squeeze every drop of life from whatever time they might have in our mortal realm. There's no finer way to embrace earthly offerings than by sampling their finest cuisine, so we've put together a mesmerizing menu that's sure to impress even the most wanton of witches. From Miss Olin Nutty Brown Bread (page 17) to "I Put a Spell on You" Brew (page 110), these enticing treats carry all the magic that their namesake curses—and clever spell-casters—hold so dear.

For those who prefer their culinary experiences to mirror the macabre, The Master's Fried Peppers (page 23) and Dead Man's Toes (page 25) will offer up a proper scare. Spicy Nightshade Stir-Fry (page 56) and Maggot-Stuffed Pork Chop (page 50) offer an exotic, earthy twist on beloved classic dishes. And our dearest Winifred would no doubt delight in serving up her Spellbook Cake (page 77)—so long as no one tries to steal it from her, of course! Throughout these pages, recipes may be marked with a few interesting runes: GF, GF*, V, V*, V+, or V+*. These runes indicate the following dietary considerations:

GF: Gluten-free

GF*: Easily adapted to be gluten-free

V: Vegetarian

V*: Easily adapted to be vegetarian

V+: Vegan

V+*: Easily adapted to be vegan

It's a *thrill* to share these otherworldly recipes for the very first time. We hope you've brought a hunger for dastardly dishes, devilish desserts, and a cupcake worthy of the black flame candle itself. So, gather your coven, summon your favorite broomstick—or vacuum—and prepare to embark upon an epicurean adventure of ghoulish proportions. After all, we only have until morning. So, come . . . we fly!

Appetizers and Sides

Winifred, Mary, and Sarah have been gone three hundred years—*right down to the day*! But now the witches are back. And their appetites are sure to be positively ghoulish. Whether you're planning a calming circle for three wayward witches or a dinner party for several hungry humans, no menu would be complete without these appetizers and sides, inspired by Salem's favorite witchy trio. From "Amok, Amok, Amok" Guacamole and Homemade Chips (page 21) to Dead Man's Toes (page 25), each of these recipes will whet the appetite of even the most ravenous of witches. Provided, of course, they don't put a spell on you, first!

Billy Butcherson Zombie Fingers

When Winifred's beau was caught sporting with her sister Sarah, he found himself in quite the pickle. Winifred's jealous streak would be Billy Butcherson's downfall . . . but it was an unfortunate incident with a manhole cover that ultimately inspired this tangy dish. Brine, garlic, and a smattering of dill create this most unusual—and decidedly delicious!—finger food.

Yield: 12 pickles | GF, V, V+

6 Persian cucumbers

12 cloves garlic, peeled

4 to 6 sprigs fresh dill

¾ cup cold water

½ cup red wine vinegar

¼ cup spicy apple cider vinegar

1 tablespoon kosher salt

¾ teaspoon sugar

½ tablespoon black peppercorns

½ teaspoon fennel seeds

½ teaspoon celery seeds

2 bay leaves

Specialty Tools

2 sealable jars, wide enough to hold 6 pickles, such as 24-ounce mason jars

Break each cucumber in half and score the nonbroken end with an X about ¼ inch deep. Gently press a clove of garlic into each scored end. Place six pieces of cucumber, standing on end with the garlic facing up, into each of two 24-ounce mason jars. They should fit snugly. Place 2 or 3 sprigs of dill in each jar. Set aside.

In a 2-cup measuring cup, combine the water, red wine vinegar, apple cider vinegar, salt, and sugar, stirring to combine. Set aside.

Warm a medium saucepan over medium heat and add the peppercorns, fennel, celery seeds, and bay leaves. Toast, moving constantly, for 2 minutes. Add the vinegar mixture and bring to a simmer. Carefully pour the hot brine into each jar, making sure that the cucumbers are covered. Make sure to get a bay leaf and about half of the spices into each jar. Add more water if needed to cover.

Seal the jars and allow them to cool to room temperature, then refrigerate. Pickles are ready to eat the next day; however, the longer they sit, the more flavorful they become. Pickles can be stored in the refrigerator for up to two months. Note that the garlic cloves may come loose from the pickles, but they can be pressed back in for serving if desired.

Appetizers & Sides

All Hallows' Eve Feast Grazing Board

According to Allison, Halloween is based on an ancient feast called All Hallows' Eve—the one night of the year when spirits can come back to roam the earth. And there's no better way to welcome ghostly guests than with this grazing board. This savory plate serves up candied clementines, kale chips, baked Brie with pesto, and the ever-appetizing "moldy" grapes. It's an ideal offering of sinister snacks for any soul feeling the slightest bit peckish—be they living . . . or deceased! Most of the components can be made in advance, but the Brie should be baked just before serving.

Yield: 6 to 8 servings | GF*, V*, V+*

For the Kale Chip Bat Wings

- 1 bunch dinosaur or Tuscan kale, washed and dried very well
- ¼ cup olive oil
- 1 tablespoon balsamic vinegar
- ½ teaspoon kosher salt
- ¼ teaspoon harissa powder

For the Candied Orange Dark Moons

- 4 clementine or mandarin oranges
- 2 cups sugar
- ½ cup bittersweet chocolate or chocolate chips

For the Moldy Grapes

- 1 bunch black globe grapes or other large grape
- ½ cup roasted salted pistachios, crushed
- 4 ounces goat cheese, slightly softened

For the Baked Swampy Brie with Pesto

- One 8-ounce wheel Brie
- 2 tablespoons homemade pesto (see page 53) or store-bought pesto
- 1 teaspoon balsamic vinegar
- 1 tablespoon shredded Parmesan cheese

For Assembly

- The Master's Fried Peppers (page 23)
- Assorted cheeses (see note)
- Assorted charcuterie (see note)
- Assorted olives and antipasto
- Jams or dips of choice
- Crackers and/or baguette slices

Notes

For the cheese, plan on 1 ounce of each cheese per person. So, if you are serving three cheeses to six people, you need 6 ounces of each cheese. For charcuterie, plan on 2 to 3 ounces per person, making sure you have that amount of each item. Since leftovers store well, feel free to make your grazing board look bountiful.

For dietary restrictions, select the items that fit your needs. The kale chips are gluten-free, vegetarian, and vegan; the moons are gluten-free and vegetarian; the grapes are gluten-free and vegetarian; and the pesto is gluten-free and vegetarian. The entire board can be made gluten-free by using gluten-free crackers and bread.

continued on page 14

Appetizers & Sides

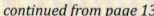
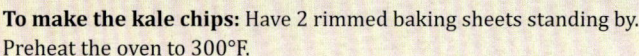

continued from page 13

To make the kale chips: Have 2 rimmed baking sheets standing by. Preheat the oven to 300°F.

To stem the kale, take each piece, fold the leaves away from the stem, and gently pull them off the stem. This will leave you with two long pieces of kale. Repeat until all the kale is stemmed and set it aside.

In a small bowl, whisk together the olive oil, vinegar, salt, and harissa. Using a pastry brush, paint a thin layer of the mixture over the surface of each baking sheet. Lay out the kale leaves in a single layer without overlapping on the baking sheets. Brush the top of each kale leaf with a light coating of the oil mixture.

Bake for 8 to 12 minutes, or until the kale is crisp but not brown. At the 8-minute mark, check carefully and pull any kale chips that are already done and rotate the pans. It is okay if the kale chips are still a bit soft in the middle; they will continue to crisp as they cool. Allow to cool completely on a baking sheet and then store in an airtight container until serving.

To make the candied oranges: Slice each orange into ¼-inch-thick slices, discarding the ends. Gently remove any seeds from each slice and discard. Set the slices aside.

In a large saucepan over medium-high heat, bring 2 cups of water to a boil and add the sugar. Stir until sugar is completely dissolved. Add the orange slices and press a piece of parchment paper down to rest on top of the oranges. Turn the heat down to low and maintain a simmer for 1 hour.

Place a wire rack set on a rimmed baking sheet. Using tongs or a slotted spoon, remove each orange slice and place it on the rack. Reserve the orange syrup for an alternate use. Allow to dry for 5 to 7 hours, or until firm and slightly tacky.

Line a baking sheet with parchment paper. In a medium microwave-safe bowl, melt the chocolate in 30-second bursts and stir until completely smooth. Do not overheat.

Dip each orange slice halfway into the chocolate, then place on the baking sheet. Refrigerate for 7 to 10 minutes, or until chocolate is set. Store in an airtight container between layers of parchment for up to three days.

To make the grapes: Remove the grapes from the stem. Place the pistachios on a shallow plate. Spread a small amount of goat cheese onto the stem end of the grape. Being a bit messy here is just fine. Roll the goat cheese in the crushed nuts. Continue until all the grapes are covered. Serve immediately or gently store in an airtight container in the refrigerator for up to one day.

Appetizers & Sides

To make the Brie: Have an oven-safe dish, large enough to hold the Brie with some room to spare, standing by. Preheat the oven to 350°F.

Using a sharp knife, score the Brie with deep cuts, about every inch all the way across, rotate the Brie, then make the same cuts across the other direction, making a crosshatch. Be careful not to cut all the way through (placing a chopstick on either side of the Brie to stop your knife can help with this). Gently open up the crosshatches a bit by bending back the wheel of Brie and then place it in the oven-safe dish. Spread the pesto over the top of the Brie, drizzle with the balsamic vinegar, and sprinkle with the Parmesan cheese. Bake for 15 to 20 minutes, or until the cheese is bubbly and gooey. Serve immediately.

To assemble: Arrange two or three cutting or serving boards on your table using risers to layer the boards. Arrange all the items using small bowls or plates to corral items such as olives, the candied oranges, The Master's Fried Peppers, jams, and dips. Kale chips, some crackers, and/or bread sticks can be served standing up in glasses or wide-mouth jars to create height. Set the cheeses with appropriate cheese knives scattered around the boards. Arrange the various charcuterie, grouped by type, directly on the board or on small plates. Tuck crackers, moldy grapes, other fruit, and baguette slices in the empty spaces. Have a heatproof spot, such as a trivet or cutting board, to place the Brie once it is out of the oven, surrounded by bread or crackers and with a serving spreader tucked in. Have small appetizer plates available for serving.

Miss Olin Nutty Brown Bread

A stickler for accuracy, Max and Allison's teacher Miss Olin holds her students to *particularly* high standards. This lover of lore appreciates attention to detail—whether she's retelling the legend of the Sanderson sisters or baking a loaf of delightful brown bread. This Miss Olin–inspired confection combines hints of hazelnut with golden raisins in a blend that is both sweet and tangy—just like the teacher herself.

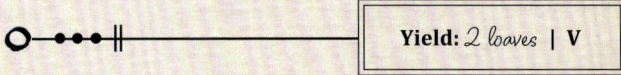

Yield: 2 loaves | V

Butter or coconut oil for greasing

3 cups whole wheat flour

1 cup all-purpose flour

½ cup dark brown sugar

1 tablespoon baking soda

1 teaspoon salt

2½ cups buttermilk

1 cup molasses

1 cup golden raisins

1 cup chopped hazelnuts

Warm softened butter or "No Witches Here" Pumpkin Butter (page 22) for serving

Preheat the oven to 350°F.

Use the butter to grease two 8-by-4-inch loaf pans and line each with a wide center strip of parchment paper that goes along the bottom and overhangs slightly from each end.

In a large bowl, mix together the whole wheat flour, all-purpose flour, brown sugar, baking soda, and salt.

In a medium bowl, whisk together the buttermilk and molasses until well combined. Stir the buttermilk mixture into the flour mixture and continue to stir until all the dry ingredients are moistened. Fold in the raisins and hazelnuts.

Split the batter between the two pans and bake for 35 to 40 minutes, or until a cake tester comes out clean. Allow to cool in the pan for 15 minutes, then use the parchment to lift the loaves and transfer them to a wire rack to cool. Serve warm with softened butter.

Leftover bread can be stored in an airtight container for up to four days. It can be served at room temperature, toasted, or rewarmed in the oven.

Pretty Black Meatball Spiders

Sarah Sanderson loves to snack on a good spider—especially the pretty ones! But when *actual* spiders aren't available, these meatball spiders make for the next best thing. Fried chow mein noodles combined with a dash of tangy mustard are sure to enchant *any* arachnid aficionado. Just watch out for those spindly legs—they've been known to tickle!

Yield: About 25 spiders

For the Spiders

- ½ cup tahini (see note)
- 3 to 5 drops black food coloring
- 1 tablespoon Worcestershire sauce
- 1 teaspoon paprika
- 2 cups packaged fried chow mein noodles, divided
- 1 pound bulk sausage
- 2 tablespoons minced shallot

For the Dipping Sauce

- ¼ cup Dijon mustard
- 1 tablespoon apple cider vinegar
- 1 tablespoon honey
- ½ tablespoon chile paste or hot sauce

Note
Have black tahini on hand? Use that and omit the food coloring!

To make the spiders: Preheat the oven to 250°F. Line two rimmed baking sheets with parchment paper.

In a small bowl, whisk together the tahini, food coloring, Worcestershire sauce, and paprika until well blended. Mix 2 tablespoons of the sauce mixture with 2 tablespoons water until well combined.

In a medium bowl, toss the thinned sauce with 1 cup of the fried noodles. Spread the noodles out in an even layer on one of the prepared baking sheets. Bake for 10 minutes, then set aside and allow to cool completely. Keep the oven on but raise the temperature to 375°F.

In a food processor, pulverize the remaining 1 cup of fried noodles into fine crumbs. Mix the remaining sauce mixture with the sausage, fried noodle crumbs, and shallot.

Form the spiders by scooping up about 2 tablespoons of the sausage mixture at a time, rolling into a ball, and inserting eight noodle "legs," four on each side. Set on the prepared baking sheets. Bake for 15 minutes, or until an instant-read thermometer inserted into the center of the spiders registers 165°F.

These can be made ahead and chilled for up to 4 hours before baking.

To make the dipping sauce: While the meatballs are baking, whisk together the mustard, vinegar, honey, and chile paste in a small bowl. Set aside until ready to serve.

Serve the meatballs warm with the dipping sauce.

Appetizers & Sides

"Amok, Amok, Amok" Guacamole and Homemade Chips

Winifred is horrified to discover that after three hundred years, All Hallows' Eve has become a night of frolic. But Sarah dances delightedly at the news. Nothing could be better than children dressing in costumes and running amok, amok, amok! Since such shenanigans require sustenance, this recipe for guacamole and homemade chips provides the perfect salty snack. While hobgoblins abound, and trusty brooms may disappear, this go-to appetizer offers a bounty of tantalizing tastes to anyone bold enough to cross paths with a witch . . . or three!

Yield: 6 servings | GF*, V*, V+*

For the Homemade Chips
- 6 sheets spring roll wrappers
- About 1 quart safflower or peanut oil for frying

For the Guacamole
- 3 ripe avocados, halved and pitted
- Juice of ½ lime
- 1 teaspoon shichimi togarashi seasoning (see note)
- 3 cloves black garlic, peeled

Note

Shichimi togarashi seasoning has bonito fish flakes, so this dish is not vegetarian or vegan. For a vegetarian option, simply omit the seasoning from the recipe, and add a pinch of red pepper flakes. To make the dish gluten-free, use regular corn chips instead of the homemade ones.

To make the chips: Cut each spring roll wrapper into strips about 1 inch wide. Pour the oil into a large heavy-bottomed pot until it reaches 3 inches deep, then place over medium-high heat until it reaches 350°F. Have a plate lined with paper towels standing by.

Fry the strips in batches using a spider or slotted spoon to turn the strips gently while they cook. Strips are ready when they are golden brown, about 1 minute. Remove the strips with the spider and place them on the prepared plate to drain. As soon as they are cool to the touch, they are ready to serve, or they can be stored in an airtight container for up to two days.

To make the guacamole: Scoop the flesh of the avocadoes into a medium serving bowl. Pour the lime juice over the avocado, sprinkle with the seasoning, and blend briefly with a fork.

On the surface of a small cutting board, with the blade of a knife facing away from you, use the flat side of the knife to smash the garlic cloves into a jam-like consistency. Scrape the garlic into the avocado mixture and use the fork to blend and incorporate it.

Serve with homemade chips.

"No Witches Here" Pumpkin Butter

When the people of Salem set out to find Thackery Binx, they pound angrily on the Sandersons' door. The villagers are on a witch hunt . . . and they're determined to reveal the true identities of the women responsible for Thackery's disappearance. But Winifred pleads ignorance, claiming "there be no witches here"—only kindly old spinster women with their cauldrons of rich, bubbling brew. Either way, the Sandersons are well-known for their sinister recipes—witchy or otherwise. And the troublesome trio wouldn't be able to resist this rich, creamy concoction. With plenty of pumpkin cooked down with sugar and spices, this pumpkin butter is the perfect complement to a loaf of Miss Olin Nutty Brown Bread (page 17) . . . and, of course, a quiet evening at home.

Yield: *About 32 ounces* | GF, V, V+

- 3 pounds winter squash, such as sugar pie, Jarrahdale, winter luxury, or butternut
- 1 cup apple juice, divided
- 2 tablespoons bourbon or vanilla extract
- 1 cup dark brown sugar
- 1 teaspoon ground cinnamon
- ¼ teaspoon ground clove

Specialty Tools
Eight 4-ounce or four 8-ounce jars

Have ready eight 4-ounce or four 8-ounce jars with tight-fitting lids, well washed or sterilized. Preheat the oven to 350°F.

Halve each squash and scoop out the seeds and stringy pulp. Cut the stem end off and discard it.

Pour ½ cup of the apple juice with ½ cup water into a roasting pan. Place the squash pieces, cut-side down, in the pan and roast for 45 to 50 minutes, or until very tender when poked with a fork.

Allow the squash to cool for 10 minutes, then use a fork and spoon to scrape the flesh from the skin. Place all the flesh and the cooking liquid in a large heavy-bottomed saucepan. Discard the skin.

Add the remaining ½ cup of apple juice, the bourbon, brown sugar, cinnamon, and clove. Place over medium heat and cook, stirring, until the mixture begins to bubble, about 10 minutes. Turn the heat down to low, cover partially, and simmer for 20 to 25 minutes, or until the mixture clings to a spoon for several seconds before falling back in the pot.

Remove from the heat and use an immersion blender to puree into a smooth texture. Immediately fill the clean jars and seal with tight-fitting lids. Allow to cool to room temperature and then refrigerate. The pumpkin butter will store in the refrigerator for up to three weeks.

Appetizers & Sides

The Master's Fried Peppers

The Sanderson sisters revere their master—that pitchfork-wielding, red-horned fellow whose dastardly tendencies often land him in hot water. But Master's spicy proclivities extend beyond mere mischief-making. With tastes that run hotter than the temperature of his abode, Master would surely find these fried peppers to be a devilish delight. No doubt, they'll keep *anyone* dancing well into the night.

Yield: 4 to 6 servings | GF, V, V+

2 tablespoons avocado oil

4 ounces shishito peppers

About 2 teaspoons black and/or red lava salt

In a medium stainless-steel or cast-iron skillet, heat the oil over high heat until it shimmers. Add the peppers and stir or shake the pan to coat the peppers in oil.

Cook, stirring or shaking the pan occasionally, for 4 to 5 minutes, until the peppers blister on all sides. Remove the pan from the heat and transfer the peppers to a serving plate.

Serve with the black and red salt in a small dish and sprinkle a few grains of salt onto each pepper just before eating.

Dead Man's Toes

'Tis time. Yes, 'tis time for a potion, forsooth!
One meant to restore sisters' glorious youth.
Flip open the book, add ingredients vile—
Toss oil and hair and red herb to the pile.
Most precious of all is the rare dead man's toe.

It needs to be fresh—so perhaps one should know
Just how to prepare it: sausage you shall need.
Add dough, an almond, and some herbs—oh, indeed
You'll find that this toe is a flavorful treat.
One certain to sweep you right off your feet.

Yield:  About 24 toes

1 pound bulk Italian sausage
1 cup panko bread crumbs
1 large egg, separated
One 17-ounce box puff pastry, thawed
24 Marcona almonds
1 tablespoon dried rosemary

Line a rimmed baking sheet with a silicone baking mat or parchment paper.

In a large bowl, combine the sausage, bread crumbs, and egg yolk. Set the egg white aside.

On a lightly floured work surface, cut each sheet of puff pastry into three 3-inch-wide strips. Roll each strip out a bit until it reaches about 12 inches in length. Cut each strip into four 3-by-3-inch squares.

Whisk the egg white with 1 teaspoon water to create an egg wash.

Brush the edges of one pastry square with the egg wash. Form about 1½ tablespoons of the sausage mixture into a rough log. Place the sausage log in the center of the pastry square, leaving a bit of sausage overhanging one end. Fold the sides of the pastry square over the sausage, overlapping in the middle, and place it, seam-side down, on the prepared baking sheet. Pinch and tuck the pastry end until it is completely closed and slightly rounded.

Egg wash the entire sausage "toe" and press one almond into the pastry end of the roll. Use a sharp knife or pastry wheel to score a knuckle toward the nail end of the toe. Sprinkle the knuckle with a few rosemary "hairs."

Repeat this process until you've used all the pastry and sausage mixture. Chill them in the refrigerator for at least 20 minutes or up to 1 hour.

Bake at 425°F for 20 to 25 minutes, or until golden brown and an instant-read thermometer inserted into the center of the sausage registers 165°F.

Appetizers & Sides

"Oh, Cheese and Crust" Homemade Crackers

In a magic-filled world, it can be difficult to keep one's head—a truth Winnie learns when an errant tree branch sends Billy Butcherson's head flying. The frustrated witch shouts, "Oh cheese and crust!" which inspires Billy to get moving. Conveniently enough, it *also* inspires this guaranteed crowd-pleaser. With hints of white cheddar and a smattering of chives, these crackers are sure to make even the surliest Sanderson take her broom to the skies in delight.

Yield: *About 72 crackers* | V

- 8 tablespoons (1 stick) unsalted butter
- 6 ounces sharp white cheddar, cut into chunks
- ¼ cup grated Parmesan cheese
- 1½ cups all-purpose flour
- 2 tablespoons heavy cream
- 1 teaspoon dried chives
- ¼ teaspoon salt

In the bowl of a food processor, combine the butter, cheddar cheese, and Parmesan cheese and pulse a few times to combine. Add the flour, heavy cream, chives, and salt and pulse until the dough just comes together. It will still be a bit crumbly.

On a cutting board, split the dough into thirds and shape each third into a log about 8 inches long. Wrap each log in parchment paper and refrigerate for at least 1 hour.

Preheat the oven to 350°F. Line a baking sheet with parchment paper or a silicone baking mat.

Slice each log into ⅛-inch-thick slices and place on the prepared baking sheet. Bake for 10 to 12 minutes, or until lightly browned and crisp. Transfer the crackers to a wire rack to cool and serve warm or at room temperature.

Dough can be kept in the refrigerator for up to three days or frozen for up to one month. If frozen, allow to defrost for 1 hour, or until it's easy to slice.

Popping Cranberries

The Sanderson sisters spend a *lot* of time crafting potions. And these popping cranberries would make an ideal ingredient for any one of the witchy sisters' bubbling brews. After a simmering syrup bath and receiving a generous sprinkle of sugar, these sweetly tart cranberries will practically pop with flavor. How *glorious*!

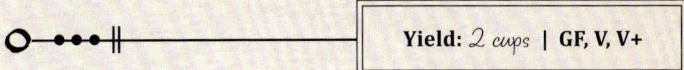

Yield: *2 cups* | GF, V, V+

- 2 cups fresh cranberries
- 2 cups granulated sugar
- 1 tablespoon fresh lemon juice
- ¾ cup superfine sugar
- ¼ teaspoon ground cinnamon

In a colander, rinse and sort the berries, removing any debris or bruised fruit. Set aside to drain.

In a large saucepan over medium-high heat, bring 2 cups of water to a boil, then turn the heat to low and add the granulated sugar, stirring until completely dissolved. Remove from the heat and add the lemon juice and cranberries. Stir to combine. Pour the mixture into a heatproof bowl and transfer to the refrigerator (covering is fine but not required). Allow to chill and infuse for 8 hours or overnight.

In a small bowl, combine the superfine sugar and cinnamon and spread it out over a large rimmed baking sheet. Strain the cranberries and reserve the liquid for future use, such as Mary's Magic Elixir (page 121). Scatter the cranberries over the baking sheet and shake the sheet back and forth to coat the berries. Allow to dry for 1 hour, or until dry.

These make a great addition to the All Hallows' Eve Feast Grazing Board (page 13), drinks as a garnish, and dessert as a topping—or simply serve them as a snack on their own. Store in an airtight container in a cool, dark place for up to one week. To gift, place in parchment-paper-lined containers and seal.

Roach Muffins

Witches have rather peculiar tastes. They think nothing of serving up a side of hag... or a spot of Dead Man's Toes (page 25). And while the mention of cockroaches might cause the occasional fainting spell, this roach-free recipe will have even mortal guests scurrying about with delight. Apples, dates, and cinnamon combine to make these muffins a perennial favorite—of witches, warlocks, and humans alike!

Yield: 12 muffins | V

1¾ cups all-purpose flour, divided

1 teaspoon baking soda

1 teaspoon baking powder

2 teaspoons ground cinnamon, divided

½ teaspoon salt

1 large apple

1 tablespoon fresh lemon juice

¼ cup sugar, plus 2 teaspoons, divided

12 ounces whole pitted dates (see note)

¼ cup boiling water

8 tablespoons (1 stick) unsalted butter, softened

½ cup dark brown sugar

2 large eggs, at room temperature

1 tablespoon vanilla extract

Note

Not a fan of bug decor? Decrease the amount of dates to 4 ounces and just add them to the batter.

Preheat the oven to 425°F. Line a 12-count muffin pan with cupcake liners.

Whisk 1½ cups of the flour, the baking soda, baking powder, 1 teaspoon of the cinnamon, and the salt together in a large bowl. Set aside.

Peel, core, and dice the apple. Place in a small bowl with the lemon juice and mix. Set aside. In a small bowl, mix 2 teaspoons of the sugar and the remaining 1 teaspoon of cinnamon together and set aside.

Reserve 12 whole dates for the garnish and finely chop the rest. In a heatproof bowl or measuring cup, cover the chopped dates with the boiling water, stir to combine, and set aside.

In a large mixing bowl using a hand mixer or in the bowl of a stand mixer fitted with the paddle attachment, beat together the butter, brown sugar, and the remaining ¼ cup of sugar on high speed until smooth and creamy, about 2 minutes. Add the eggs and vanilla. Beat on medium speed for 1 minute, then turn to high speed and beat until the mixture is combined and mostly creamy. (It's okay if it appears somewhat curdled.) With the mixer running on low speed, add the flour mixture and continue to mix until it is incorporated. Fold in the dates with their liquid.

Toss the apples with the remaining ¼ cup of flour and fold the apple mixture into the batter. Fill each muffin liner two-thirds of the way full and top with about ¼ teaspoon of the cinnamon sugar for each muffin.

Bake for 5 minutes at 425°F, then, keeping the muffins in the oven, reduce the oven temperature to 350°F. Bake for 12 to 15 minutes more, or until a toothpick inserted in the center comes out clean.

While the muffins are baking, prepare the cockroach garnish. Take each reserved whole date and make a cut down the top center, starting at the hole. Leave ½ inch uncut at the other end. Next, cut the same line, about ½ inch to the left and right of the center cut, creating two wings. Gently lift the wings away from the body and pose as desired. As soon as the muffins come out of the oven, place one date roach on each muffin, securing with a toothpick if desired.

Pastry Boots

Winnie, Mary, and Sarah eagerly embrace their witchy wardrobe. With flowing gowns, bristly brooms, and of course, their trademark jet-black boots, the Sandersons make for the picture-perfect witches. These black puff pastry boots evoke the essence of the sisters—while offering up a savory twist. Stuffed with spinach, feta, and a hint of bell pepper, these pastries are sure to kick any menu up a notch.

Yield: About 24 boots | V

- 1 tablespoon olive oil
- 2 tablespoons salted butter
- 2 cloves garlic, minced
- 1 yellow bell pepper, diced
- One 16-ounce package frozen spinach, thawed and drained
- Two 17-ounce packages frozen puff pastry sheets
- 6 ounces feta cheese crumbles
- 2 egg whites
- 2 to 3 drops black food coloring

Specialty Tools
Boot-shaped cookie cutter

Note
Want to make these ahead? Assemble the boots as above and instead of chilling in the refrigerator, freeze on the baking sheets until solid, about 1 hour. Then transfer to an airtight container and continue to freeze until needed, for up to one month. Bake as directed above, but note that the pastry may need a few extra minutes to cook.

In a large skillet over medium heat, add the olive oil and butter. When butter begins to foam, add the garlic, stir for 1 minute until fragrant, then add the bell pepper. Stir to coat and cook for 2 to 3 minutes more, until just barely tender. Pull out 24 pieces of bell pepper and reserve in a small bowl. Stir in the spinach and cook for 1 to 2 more minutes. Remove from the heat, transfer to a bowl, and allow to cool.

While the spinach mixture is cooling, defrost the puff pastry according to package directions. Once the spinach mixture is cool to the touch, stir in the feta and set aside.

Line two baking sheets with parchment paper or silicone baking mats. In a small bowl, whisk the egg whites with 2 tablespoons of water until frothy, add the food coloring, and stir to combine.

On a lightly floured surface and working with one piece of puff pastry at a time, roll out the pastry to about ¼-inch thickness. Use a boot-shaped cookie cutter to cut out pairs of boots. Place half of the boots on one prepared baking sheet and spread a heaping tablespoon of filling onto each boot, leaving a blank border around the edge. Place another boot on top of the filling, stretching gently if needed, and use a fork to crimp the edges closed. Using a pastry brush, brush the whole boot with the egg wash, prick the boot (at the bottom of the shaft) with the tines of the fork, and cover the holes with a reserved piece of bell pepper to create the buckle. Once the baking sheet is full, transfer it to the refrigerator and chill for at least 20 minutes.

Preheat the oven to 425°F.

Continue to make more boots by rolling out the other pieces of puff pastry one at a time and repeating the above steps.

Bake the pastries, rotating the sheets halfway through baking, for 15 to 20 minutes, or until golden brown and crisp. Allow to cool for 5 minutes before serving. Serve warm or at room temperature. Pastries can be stored in an airtight container in the refrigerator for up to three days and reheated in a 350°F oven for 10 minutes.

Appetizers & Sides

Main Dishes

After whetting their appetites, Salem's beloved witches will no doubt be ready for a proper feast. These main dishes are inspired by the Sanderson sisters' spells, Max and Dani's home-cooked meals, and the very flavors of fall themselves. They're sure to be the hit of any All Hallows' Eve event, or even just a quiet evening in with Master. And they're just the thing to give any partygoer the energy to dance until dawn . . . or until Winifred's spell is finally broken!

Mrs. Dennison's Roasted Pumpkin Tacos

In California, where the Dennisons are from, tacos are a staple. And this pumpkin-based meal provides a Halloween twist on a Hollywood classic, something Mrs. Dennison would surely make for Max and Dani during their transition to Salem. Roasted vegetables, savory spices, and the most quintessential of fall foods come together to make this meal an instant favorite. With sun-hued tones that evoke an air of serenity, this dish is perfect to serve at your next family dinner. You see, they're very health-conscious in Los Angeles . . . and Mrs. Dennison's tacos are the perfect way to bring a slice of California—and one of Salem, too!—into your own home.

Yield: 4 servings | GF*, V, V+*

For the Pumpkin Tacos
1 tablespoon olive oil

1 teaspoon adobo sauce (from canned chipotles in adobo)

Juice of ½ lime

½ teaspoon salt

½ teaspoon dried Mexican oregano

¼ teaspoon ground cinnamon

2 pounds winter squash, such as sugar pie, acorn, butternut, or kabocha, peeled, seeded, and sliced into 2-inch strips

For the Corn Salad
1 tablespoon vegetable oil

1 chipotle pepper in adobo sauce, drained and diced

4 cups fresh or thawed frozen corn kernels

½ teaspoon salt

1 cup picked fresh cilantro leaves

½ red onion, diced

Juice of ½ lime

For the Refried Black Beans
2 tablespoons salted butter

Two 15-ounce cans black beans, liquid reserved from 1 can

1 bay leaf

½ teaspoon salt

¼ teaspoon garlic powder

¼ teaspoon ground coriander

For Assembly
8 corn tortillas

Shredded cabbage (optional)

Cotija cheese (optional)

Crema (optional)

continued on page 36

Note
This recipe can be easily made gluten-free and vegan by swapping the butter for coconut oil, swapping the Cotija cheese for a vegan cheese, omitting the crema, and using gluten-free tortillas.

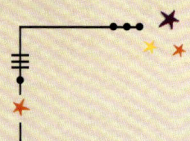

continued from page 35

To make the pumpkin tacos: Preheat the oven to 400°F.

In a large bowl, combine the olive oil, adobo sauce, lime juice, salt, oregano, and cinnamon. Whisk to combine. Add the pumpkin slices and toss to coat thoroughly. Arrange the pumpkin slices in a single layer on a rimmed baking sheet and roast for 15 to 20 minutes, or until tender and starting to caramelize.

While the pumpkin is roasting, make the corn salad and black beans.

To make the corn salad: In a large sauté pan over medium heat, combine the oil and the chipotle. Sauté for 2 to 3 minutes, until fragrant and sticky. Add the corn and salt to the pan and stir to coat. Continue to sauté, stirring occasionally, until the corn is starting to brown in places, 7 to 10 minutes. Transfer the corn to a large bowl. Roughly chop the cilantro leaves and add them to the corn along with the onion and lime juice. Stir to combine and set aside until serving.

To make the black beans: In the same sauté pan (now with browned chipotle bits) over medium heat, melt the butter until it foams. Add the beans and the reserved liquid of one can. Fill the can halfway with water and add it to the beans. Add the bay leaf, salt, garlic powder, and coriander, stirring to combine.

Bring the beans to a low boil, then turn down the heat to low and simmer for 10 to 15 minutes, until most of the liquid has been reduced. Remove from the heat and use the back of a wooden spoon to smash most of the beans. Stir to combine. Keep warm until serving.

To assemble: In a lightly greased pan over medium-high heat, warm each tortilla for 1 to 2 minutes per side. Smear each tortilla with black beans, then add corn salad and three to four slices of pumpkin. Top with cabbage, cotija cheese, and/or crema (if using). Alternatively, warm all the tortillas and keep them warm in a tortilla warmer. Set up all the components as a taco bar and allow guests to assemble their own.

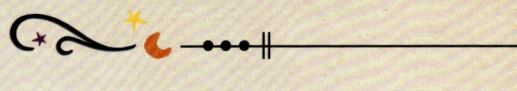

Shishkebaby

When Dani finds herself facing her soon-to-be nemeses, she puts on her bravest face and pretends to be a witch herself. Dani clings to her false alias, even when Mary pokes at her and declares her to be a well-fed "shishkebaby." In this play on Dani's unwanted nickname, speared cauliflower, peppers, and onions are seasoned with balsamic vinegar, olive oil, and salt, creating a burst of roasted flavor that's delightfully bold—just like Dani herself.

Yield: 8 servings as a main course or up to 16 as an appetizer | GF, V, V+

For the Marinade
Juice and zest of 1 orange
¼ cup balsamic vinegar
½ cup olive oil
1 teaspoon kosher salt
1 teaspoon fresh ground black pepper

For the Skewers
1 bunch (about 1 pound) rainbow carrots
1 pound 1-inch creamer potatoes
2 pounds mini sweet peppers
1 head Roman cauliflower, broken into bite-size florets
One 14-ounce bag frozen pearl onions, thawed

Specialty Tools
Thirty-two 10-inch bamboo skewers

To make the marinade: In a medium bowl, whisk together the orange juice and zest, balsamic vinegar, olive oil, salt, and black pepper. Set aside.

To make the skewers: Preheat the oven to 375°F and have two rimmed baking sheets standing by.

Halve the carrots lengthwise. Cut each half, at an angle, into ½-inch slices. Alternating vegetables, load up each skewer with at least one piece each of carrot, potato, sweet pepper, cauliflower, and onion, doubling up on smaller ones, such as onion and carrot. Continue until all the skewers are complete. Any extra vegetables can be roasted separately or saved for another use.

Line up the skewers in a single layer on each baking sheet, drizzle with the marinade, and shake to coat. You may not need all the marinade. Let stand for 10 minutes, then roast for 20 to 25 minutes, or until the potatoes are fork-tender and vegetables are well browned.

As a main dish, serve over rice or noodles drizzled with any remaining marinade. As an appetizer, serve warm or at room temperature drizzled with any remaining marinade.

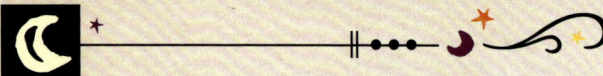

Knockout Skillet French Toast

Allison doesn't pull any punches when it comes to protecting Dani. When she sees what the witches have in store, the brave young Salemite grabs a frying pan and wallops Mary, knocking the witch out just long enough for Dani to run away. Just like its namesake, this dish is sure to knock the socks off even the pickiest eaters. Custard-coated bread picks up hints of brown sugar, cinnamon, and apples as it crisps in a buttery skillet. It's the perfect way to kick off time spent catching up with—or digging up!—old friends.

Yield: 4 servings | GF*, V

- ½ cup golden brown sugar
- Juice of 1 lemon
- ½ teaspoon ground cinnamon
- 2 apples
- 5 tablespoons salted butter, divided
- Six ½-inch slices brioche or buttermilk bread
- ½ cup whole milk
- ½ cup heavy cream
- 3 large eggs
- ½ cup chopped walnuts or pecans (optional)

Note: This recipe can be easily made gluten-free by using your favorite gluten-free bread.

In a medium bowl, mix together the sugar, lemon juice, and cinnamon. Core and slice each apple, adding the slices to the bowl and stirring to coat. Let the apples macerate in the mixture for 5 to 10 minutes.

In a 10-inch cast-iron or ovenproof skillet over medium-high heat, melt 2 tablespoons of the butter until it foams. Add the apples and all their juices. Simmer the apples until just tender, about 5 minutes. Remove from the heat and use a slotted spoon to remove the apples from the juices and set aside.

Return the skillet to medium-high heat and simmer the juices until they reduce enough to coat the back of a spoon, 3 to 5 minutes. Transfer to a heatproof container and set aside.

In a large bowl big enough to dunk the slices of bread, whisk together the milk, cream, and eggs, then set aside.

Heat 1 tablespoon of the butter in the skillet until it foams. Place two pieces of bread in the skillet and brown for about 1 minute on each side. Repeat with the remaining 2 tablespoons of butter and slices of bread until all six slices have been browned on both sides. Remove the pan from the heat.

Preheat the oven to 350°F.

Dunk each piece of bread into the egg custard and place it in the skillet. Tuck apple slices in between each piece of bread. Stagger the top layer, tucking apples into the nooks. Pour the remaining custard into the pan. Let the bread absorb the custard while the oven preheats. Bake for 25 to 30 minutes, until a knife inserted into the center comes out clean. Sprinkle the top with the walnuts (if using) in the last 10 minutes of baking.

Serve with the reserved apple syrup.

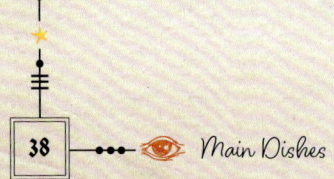

Full Moon Blue Cheese Onion Tart

Magic is at its most powerful at the full moon. It's these nights when witches fly broomsticks—or vacuums—across starlit skies, and the veil between two worlds grows precariously thin. It's *also* the perfect time to bake this tart. This dish pairs blue cheese with caramelized onions, creating a cheesy, savory delicacy that's revered in this realm . . . and beyond.

Yield: 6 servings as a main course or up to 10 as an appetizer | V

For the Crust
- 1¼ cups all-purpose flour
- ½ teaspoon salt
- 4 tablespoons unsalted butter, very cold
- 2 tablespoons solid vegetable shortening, very cold
- 4 tablespoons ice water
- 1 egg white
- Dried herbs, such as rosemary, for decorations (optional)
- Black food coloring (optional)

For the Filling
- 1½ tablespoons olive oil
- 1 tablespoon salted butter
- 2 yellow onions, thinly sliced
- ½ teaspoon kosher salt
- 3 sprigs fresh thyme
- ½ teaspoon fresh ground black pepper
- 8 ounces cream cheese, softened
- 4 ounces blue cheese, crumbled
- ¼ cup sour cream
- 1 large egg
- 2 tablespoons all-purpose flour

Specialty Tools
- 9-inch tart pan
- Broom- and bat-shaped cookie cutters (optional)
- Pie weights or dried beans

To make the crust: Have a 9-inch tart pan standing by. In a large bowl, combine the flour and salt. Using a pastry cutter or two forks, cut the butter and shortening into the flour until the mixture is sandy without any pieces larger than a pea. Slowly add the ice water and continue to gently work the mixture just until the dough comes together. You may need a bit more water.

On a lightly floured surface, roll out the dough into a 12-inch circle. Fit the dough into the tart pan by gently pressing it to the bottom and into the sides. Use a knife to remove the excess dough. Chill the tart pan in the refrigerator for at least 30 minutes. While the dough is chilling, preheat the oven to 400°F.

If creating the decorations, reroll the excess dough to ¼-inch thickness and use the cookie cutters to cut out brooms and bats. Place them on a baking sheet and refrigerate until needed.

Remove the tart pan from the refrigerator. Prepare the dough for blind baking by lining it with two pieces of overlapping aluminum foil so that the entire crust is covered. Fill the center of the tart shell with pie weights. Bake for 10 minutes.

While the crust is baking, prepare an egg wash by combining the egg white with 1 tablespoon water and whisking until frothy.

At the 10-minute mark, remove the tart shell from the oven, carefully lift out the foil and weights, and set aside. Brush the whole tart shell with the egg wash and return to the oven for 5 to 7 minutes more, or until just golden brown. Remove from the oven and set aside.

continued on page 42

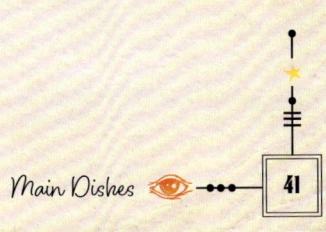

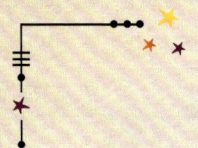

continued from page 41

To finish the decorations, brush the broom shapes with egg wash and add some dried herbs (if using) to create the end of the broom. Add a few drops of black food coloring (if using) to the remaining egg wash and brush the bat shapes. Bake for 5 to 7 minutes, or until crisp. Allow to cool completely and store in an airtight container until needed.

To make the filling: Heat the oil and butter in a medium pan over medium-high heat until the butter foams. Add the onions and toss to coat with oil and butter. Sprinkle the salt evenly across the onions, turn the heat to medium-low, add the thyme sprigs, and cook, stirring frequently, until the onions are soft and fully caramelized, about 20 minutes. Remove the thyme sprigs and discard. Season with the black pepper, then set aside.

Preheat the oven to 350°F.

In a medium bowl using a hand mixer on medium speed, beat the cream cheese until smooth. Add the blue cheese, sour cream, egg, and flour. Beat again on medium speed until the mixture is thoroughly combined and mostly smooth with some chunks of blue cheese. Set aside.

To assemble, spread the onions in an even layer on the bottom of the crust. With a large spoon, drop large dollops of filling across the onions and smooth out in an even layer. Bake for 20 to 25 minutes, or until the top is golden brown.

Cool for 10 minutes, decorate with the pastry brooms and bats, and serve.

===== Notes =====

The tart shell and decorations can be made up to a day ahead and stored in an airtight container until needed.

This dish pairs well with a green salad or sliced thin as part of the All Hallows' Eve Feast Grazing Board (page 13).

Main Dishes

Main Dishes

Mummy's Scorpion Pie

Winifred, Mary, and Sarah have fond memories of the woman who brought them into the world. Mummy taught them everything she knew—and instilled in them a fondness for her beloved Scorpion Pie. With butter, crabmeat, and corn, this dish is best served with a side of nostalgia. It's perfect for sharing at a family gathering, a séance, and of course, your next calming circle.

Yield: 4 servings

1½ pounds whole crab (see note)

1 tablespoon olive oil, divided

Kernels from 2 corncobs or 1 cup thawed frozen corn

2 tablespoons unsalted butter

1 small white onion, diced

3 or 4 stalks celery, preferably from the heart with leaves

2 tablespoons all-purpose flour

1 teaspoon kosher salt

1 pound new potatoes, quartered

2 cups vegetable broth

Zest and juice of 1 lemon, separated

2 tablespoons minced fresh parsley

1 tablespoon minced fresh dill

1 large egg

14 ounces frozen puff pastry, thawed and standing by in the refrigerator

Specialty Tools
Four 16-ounce oven-safe bowls

If using whole crab, remove all the crabmeat from its shell, making sure to get the claw meat. Reserve some of the larger shell pieces to add to the broth and save four of the walking (side) legs for garnish. These will be your "scorpion stingers." Refrigerate until needed.

In a large pot or Dutch oven over medium-high heat, place ½ tablespoon of the olive oil and the corn in a single layer. Leave undisturbed for 1 to 2 minutes, then stir and continue to cook, stirring only occasionally, until the corn begins to brown, about 5 minutes.

Transfer the corn to a plate—it's fine to leave a few kernels behind—and set aside. Add the remaining ½ tablespoon of olive oil and the butter and heat until the butter foams. Add the onion, stir to coat, and sauté for 1 to 2 minutes. Add the celery and sauté 3 to 5 minutes more, or until the onion and celery soften.

Add the flour and salt, stir again, and cook for 1 to 2 minutes, or until the flour smells nutty. Add the potatoes and stir to coat. Add the broth and reserved pieces of crab shell, if using. Bring to a simmer, then turn the heat to low and add the lemon zest. Simmer for 10 minutes, or until the potatoes are just tender. Remove from the heat and remove and discard the crab shell. Stir in the corn, lemon juice, parsley, dill, and crabmeat.

Preheat the oven to 425°F.

Meanwhile, in a small bowl, whisk together the egg with 1 tablespoon water to make an egg wash. Split the filling mixture between four 16-ounce oven-safe bowls, filling them almost to the top.

continued on page 46

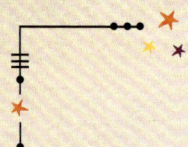

continued from page 45

Cut 1-inch-wide strips of puff pastry. Using a pastry brush, brush the edges of the bowls with the egg wash, then begin layering the strips across each bowl. The strips should overhang the edge of the bowl by about ¼ inch on either side. Trim as necessary. Brush each strip with egg wash before adding the additional strips. Continue until the surfaces of the bowls have been covered in pastry. Fold the edges toward the center of the bowls and press down gently to adhere to the edge. Create the "stinger" by tucking a reserved crab leg, if using, into the pastry at one end of the bowl.

Bake for 15 to 20 minutes, or until the pastry is puffed and golden brown. Allow to cool for 5 minutes before serving. Caution: The filling will be hot!

> **Note**
>
> Crab is normally sold live or cooked, with the latter being the most common at your local market. Your seafood counter should be able to crack and clean your crab for you, but you may need to ask them to do it. This makes prep at home much easier. If whole crab is not available, purchase 1 cup (about 10 ounces) of crabmeat.

Main Dishes

"Who's Going for the Jacuzzi" Lobster

With the Sandersons chasing them down, Max, Allison, and Dani hide in a back alley. As they cower beside a lobster tank—and watch in silence while a jovial cook asks an unfortunate crustacean, "Who's going for the Jacuzzi?"—the kids furiously plot to get the witches into hot water. Inspired by their Jacuzzi-bound friend, this meal pairs succulent seasonings with a generous dollop of butter. Rich, savory, and always appetizing, this lobster is sure to please even the crabbiest of crowds.

Yield: 2 servings | GF*

- 6 tablespoons salted butter, divided
- 3 cloves garlic, peeled
- ½ cup packed parsley leaves
- Zest of 1 lemon
- ½ cup shredded Parmesan cheese
- ½ cup fine plain bread crumbs
- Four 3- to 5-ounce raw lobster tails
- ½ cup white wine
- 1 bunch asparagus, snapped
- 1 tablespoon olive oil
- ½ teaspoon kosher salt

> **Note**
> This recipe can be easily made gluten-free by using gluten-free bread crumbs, gluten-free panko, or even crushed almonds.

In a small microwave-safe bowl or small saucepan, melt 4 tablespoons of the butter and set aside to cool.

In the bowl of a food processor, pulse together the garlic and parsley until finely chopped. Add the lemon zest and Parmesan cheese and pulse again until the mixture is sandy. Add the bread crumbs and pulse just to combine. Transfer the mixture to a medium bowl and stir in the melted butter.

Preheat the oven to 425°F.

Using kitchen shears, cut the shell on the underside of each lobster tail down the center, leaving the tail fan intact. Remove any swimmerets as well. Holding each tail, cut facing up, and bend away from you, loosening the meat. Gently pull the tail meat out of the shell, being careful to leave it attached to the tail fan, and bring it back down to rest on the shell beneath. The meat should look like it is riding piggyback on its shell. Repeat with the remaining three tails.

Grease a baking dish with the remaining 2 tablespoons of butter and pour in the white wine.

Place the tails in the baking dish and divide the crumb mixture evenly between them. Press the mixture onto the lobster meat, completely coating it.

Place the asparagus on a rimmed baking sheet, drizzle with the olive oil, and sprinkle the salt over the stalks. Shake the pan to coat.

Bake the lobster tails and the asparagus for 8 minutes. Remove the asparagus, turn the broiler to high, and broil for 2 minutes, or until bread crumbs are brown.

Serve immediately with the lobster tails plated over a grid of the asparagus and drizzle with the juices from the bottom of the lobster pan.

Main Dishes

Spicy Cauliflower Ears

It's a little-known fact that a witch's curse cannot take hold if its victim never hears it. When the Sanderson sisters begin to sing, Thackery's dad warns the villagers, "Listen to them not!" And again three hundred years later when Winnie, Mary, and Sarah burst into a more *robust* song, Dani screams for everyone to cover their ears. These cauliflower ears—covered in a tasty, buffalo wing sauce—are a vegetarian twist on a tangy classic. But watch out—*they* might just put a spell on you!

Yield: 4 servings as a main course or up to 8 as an appetizer | GF*, V, V+

¾ cup all-purpose flour

½ teaspoon salt

1 teaspoon garlic powder

1 teaspoon smoked paprika

Fresh ground black pepper

1 cup oat or other plant-based milk

1 cauliflower head, broken into bite-size florets

1½ cups panko bread crumbs

Homemade barbecue sauce (page 65)

Notes

Serve with extra barbecue sauce and/or your favorite wing dip!

This recipe can be easily made gluten-free by using a gluten-free flour, such as rice or chickpea, and omitting or using gluten-free panko bread crumbs.

Line a rimmed baking sheet with parchment paper and preheat the oven to 375°F.

In a large bowl, combine the flour, salt, garlic powder, and paprika. Season with black pepper to taste and stir to combine. Add the oat milk and stir until well combined, noting that some lumps are okay. Add the cauliflower and stir until the florets are well coated in the batter.

Working in batches, place about ½ cup of bread crumbs in a small bowl and add the florets in small batches. Toss to coat and place the coated florets on the prepared baking sheet. Repeat with the remaining bread crumbs and florets, keeping them in a single layer on the baking sheet.

Bake for 20 minutes, remove from the oven, and drizzle with the barbecue sauce. Use a spatula to turn the florets and coat thoroughly with the sauce. Reserve the remaining sauce for serving. Return the cauliflower to the oven and bake for 15 to 20 minutes more, or until the florets are fork-tender and the glaze is set and starting to brown.

Roasted Red Spice Chicken

Winifred Sanderson has been called many things—but bland is most definitely *not* one of them. This chicken dish conjures her spicy essence, with its combination of heat-inducing herbs and a fiery harissa rub. As the witch herself once said while trapped inside a prison for children, "Hot! Hot!"

Yield: *6 servings* | **GF**

- 3 or 4 sprigs fresh oregano, gently crushed
- 6 cloves garlic, smashed
- ½ cup avocado or olive oil
- ½ cup apple cider vinegar
- 2 tablespoons pomegranate syrup or molasses
- 4 teaspoons harissa powder or paste
- 1½ teaspoons kosher salt
- ½ teaspoon ground sumac
- 3 pounds boneless skinless chicken thighs

In a container that seals well, combine the oregano, garlic, oil, vinegar, syrup, harissa, salt, and sumac. Stir well to combine. Add the chicken pieces to the marinade and make sure they are coated well. Marinate in the refrigerator for at least 30 minutes or up to 2 hours.

To grill the chicken, heat a grill to about 375°F. Grill the chicken, turning at least once, for 7 to 10 minutes, or until an instant-read thermometer inserted into the thickest part of the meat registers 165°F.

Alternatively, bake the chicken. Preheat the oven and a rimmed baking sheet to 375°F. Place the chicken in a single layer on the preheated baking sheet and bake for 5 minutes. Flip the thighs and bake for 3 to 5 minutes more, or until an instant-read thermometer inserted into the thickest part of the meat registers 165°F.

Note

If you prefer bone-in, skin-on chicken, this marinade still works well, but allow about 30 more minutes for cooking.

Maggot-Stuffed Pork Chop

Billy Butcherson may be a "maggoty mouth peasant"—at least according to Winifred. After all, he *has* been buried for centuries . . . and he almost definitely was caught sporting with the wrong Sanderson sister. But whatever else Billy may be, he would most certainly be a lover of this pork chop—or, he *would* have been . . . before his mouth was sewn shut by that woefully wounded Winifred!

Yield: 4 servings

For the Spaetzle Maggots

- 1 cup all-purpose flour
- 1 teaspoon salt, plus more for boiling
- ¼ teaspoon white pepper
- ½ teaspoon ground nutmeg
- ¼ cup half-and-half
- 2 large eggs
- 4 tablespoons unsalted butter, melted

For the Pork Chops

- 4 thick-cut boneless pork chops (about 2 pounds)
- 2 teaspoons salt
- 2 teaspoons vegetable oil
- 2 tablespoons unsalted butter

For the Apples and Assembly

- ¼ cup apple cider vinegar
- 1 large apple, cored and chopped into 1-inch pieces
- ½ teaspoon dried thyme
- 1 cup packed fresh parsley leaves, roughly chopped (optional)

Specialty Tools

Spaetzle maker or flat cheese grater

To make the maggots: In a medium bowl, mix together the flour, salt, white pepper, and nutmeg. In a separate small bowl, whisk together the half-and-half and eggs. Make a well in the flour mixture, add the egg mixture, and stir to combine.

Allow the batter to rest while bringing a large pot of salted water to a boil and placing the melted butter in a large bowl.

When the water is boiling, turn the heat to medium and maintain a low boil. Use a spaetzle maker or flat cheese grater to press the batter through, a small portion at a time, into the boiling water. Cook for 2 to 3 minutes, or until all the dumplings are floating. Remove from the water with a spider or large strainer, transfer to the melted butter, and stir to combine.

Continue this process until all the spaetzle batter has been used. Make sure the spaetzle is well coated in butter and set aside.

To make the pork chops: Preheat the oven to 350°F.

Cut a deep slit about 3 inches long into the thick side of each pork chop, being careful not to pierce through to the other side. Season the inside and outside with the salt. In a large oven-safe skillet over medium-high heat, combine the vegetable oil and butter and heat until the butter foams. Add the pork chops and brown on each side without disturbing for 3 to 4 minutes. Transfer the browned pork chops to an oven-safe casserole dish. Cover with aluminum foil and cook for 10 to 15 minutes, or until an instant-read thermometer inserted into the thickest part of the meat registers 145°F. Allow to rest 3 to 5 minutes.

continued on page 52

Main Dishes

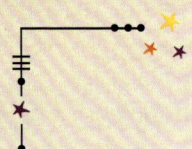

continued from page 50

To make the apples and assemble: While the pork finishes cooking in the oven, deglaze the skillet over medium-high heat with the apple cider vinegar, stirring for 2 to 3 minutes. Add the apples and thyme and cook the apples until most of the liquid has been absorbed and the apples are tender, about 7 minutes.

Add the spaetzle, stir to make sure everything is well coated, and sauté for 3 to 5 minutes more, continuing to stir so the spaetzle does not stick.

Stuff each pork chop with the spaetzle mixture by using tongs to stand the pork chop on the intact edge. Plate each stuffed chop on top of more of the spaetzle mixture. Scatter the parsley (if using) over each plate.

Main Dishes

Green Mummy Roll Ups

Halloween conjures a bounty of images—jack-o'-lanterns, black flame candles, and of course, *mummies*. These zucchini-based rolls might seem a bit greener than their white-wrapped bipedal brethren, but their mozzarella filling is packed with frightfully fabulous flavors. Bone-*appétit*!

Yield: 4 to 6 servings | GF, V

For the Pesto

- 3 large cloves garlic, smashed
- ½ cup toasted walnuts (see note)
- 1 cup packed fresh basil leaves
- 1 cup packed fresh parsley leaves
- ½ cup shredded Parmesan cheese
- ¼ cup olive oil
- ¼ cup heavy cream
- ½ teaspoon salt
- Fresh ground black pepper
- Juice of ½ lemon

For the Roll Ups

- 16 ounces low-moisture ricotta cheese
- ½ teaspoon salt
- Fresh ground black pepper
- 1 large egg
- 2 cups shredded mozzarella cheese, divided
- ½ cup shredded Parmesan cheese
- 2 large zucchinis
- 4 to 6 Kalamata olives, sliced (optional)

To make the pesto: In the bowl of a food processor, pulse the garlic a few times until roughly chopped. Add the walnuts, pulse again, then add the basil and parsley leaves. Run the food processor until everything is finely chopped, about 30 seconds.

Add the Parmesan cheese, then run the food processor again until everything comes together as a paste, about 30 seconds.

With the machine running, add the olive oil in a slow stream until it is completely incorporated. Stop the machine and scrape down the sides. With the machine running, add the heavy cream slowly until it is completely incorporated. Add the salt and season with black pepper to taste. Pulse again to combine. Add the lemon juice, run the food processor another 30 seconds, and then set the pesto aside.

To make the roll ups: Preheat the oven to 400°F. In a large bowl, mix together the ricotta cheese, salt, black pepper to taste, egg, 1 cup of the mozzarella cheese, and the Parmesan cheese. Set aside.

Using a wide vegetable peeler, peel off most of the dark green skin of each zucchini and discard. Continue to peel each zucchini in wide ribbons until you begin to reach the seeds. Set all the ribbons aside. Quarter the core of each zucchini and dice into ¼-inch pieces.

In a 9-by-13-inch casserole pan, spread half of the pesto mixture on the bottom of the pan.

continued on page 55

Note

To toast the walnuts, heat a small stainless-steel or cast-iron pan on the stove over medium-high heat for about 1 minute. Add the nuts, stir, and then remove the pan from the heat. Continue to stir the nuts until fragrant, about 2 minutes.

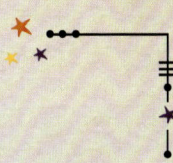

continued from page 53

On a work surface, layer four to six zucchini ribbons, slightly overlapping, to create a "sheet" of zucchini. Lay another two strips vertically down the center of the sheet so their ends stick out past the top and bottom of the sheet. Place about 4 tablespoons of the ricotta mixture in the center of the sheet and form it into a log shape down the center.

Pull the top and bottom overhanging pieces toward the center to help close the ends. Fold each side ribbon of zucchini toward the center, overlapping and alternating, to create a mummied effect. Once the filling is all wrapped up, make eyes by tucking two olive slices (if using) into the top of the mummy. Use a spatula to transfer the completed mummy to the casserole pan. Repeat with the remaining zucchini ribbons until filling is all used. Leave about 1 inch in between each mummy.

Mix the cubed zucchini with the remaining pesto and scatter it in between and around each mummy. Bake for 15 to 20 minutes, until bubbling and beginning to brown.

Remove from the oven and sprinkle the remaining 1 cup of mozzarella cheese on each mummy. Return to the oven. Bake for 15 minutes more, or until the mozzarella is bubbly and brown.

Spicy Nightshade Stir-Fry

All Hallows' Eve—that trick-filled night
When ghouls descend to give a fright.
And costumed children fill the streets
To reap their share of tricks—or treats!
Before the fun gets underway,

One must fill up—so one can play!
This nightshade stir-fry's sure to please,
With garlic, ginger, and veggies.
So, fill those plates up good and high.
Eat up! Because tonight, we fly!

Yield: 4 servings | GF*, V, V+*

For the Sauce

1 tablespoon grated fresh ginger

4 cloves garlic, minced

¼ cup soy sauce

1 teaspoon sesame oil

1 teaspoon chile-garlic sauce

1 teaspoon cornstarch

For the Stir-Fry

3 tablespoons peanut oil, divided (or other high-smoke-point oil)

1 yellow onion, thinly sliced

2 orange bell peppers, cut into thin strips

12 small cremini mushrooms, halved (see note)

1 Chinese eggplant, halved lengthwise, then sliced into half-moons

¼ teaspoon kosher salt

Cooked rice or noodles for serving

4 green onions, white and light green parts only, sliced (optional)

½ cup roasted salted cashews, roughly chopped (optional)

To make the sauce: In a small bowl, combine the ginger, garlic, soy sauce, sesame oil, and chile-garlic sauce. Set aside. In another small bowl, make a slurry by whisking together the cornstarch and 2 tablespoons water. Set aside.

To make the stir-fry: In a large wok or high-sided sauté pan over medium-high heat, heat half of the oil until it shimmers. Add the onion and cook, stirring continuously, until it is translucent and begins to brown, 3 to 4 minutes. Add the bell peppers, stir to combine, and cook 3 to 4 minutes more, until the peppers soften slightly and brown in some spots.

Using tongs, transfer the peppers and onions to a plate. Add the remaining half of the oil and heat until it shimmers. Add the mushrooms and eggplant, stirring to combine. Cook for 4 to 5 minutes, until browning and softened. Add the peppers and onions back to the pan, add the sauce, and stir to combine. Cook for 1 to 2 minutes, then add the cornstarch slurry. Stir to combine and cook for 1 to 2 minutes more, until the sauce thickens.

Serve over rice or noodles with the green onions and cashews as a garnish (if using).

Notes

Want to turn your mushrooms into ghouls? Leave them whole and use a straw to poke out two holes for the eyes. Use a paring knife to carve a line to create the mouth. Sauté them whole with the eggplant.

This recipe can be made gluten-free and vegan by swapping out the soy sauce for a gluten-free vegan version and serving with rice.

Waterwheel Pot Pie

The waterwheel at the Sanderson homestead served as a pillar of the original Salem community. And while it turned for many years, its gears eventually slowed . . . as did the caretakers who so lovingly maintained it. With this pot pie, Salem's relic need not be forgotten. Simply line a dish with pastry, fill it with vegetables, and delight in this time-honored piece of Salem's history.

Yield: 6 servings | V

For the Crust

2½ cups all-purpose flour

1 teaspoon salt

8 tablespoons (1 stick) unsalted butter, very cold, divided

¼ cup solid vegetable shortening, very cold

⅓ cup ice water

For the Filling

2 tablespoons vegetable oil

2 tablespoons salted butter

2 leeks, well washed and trimmed, sliced

4 to 6 stalks celery, preferably from the heart with leaves, sliced

1 teaspoon salt

½ teaspoon ground sumac

½ teaspoon dried thyme

¼ teaspoon white pepper

2 tablespoons all-purpose flour

2 cups vegetable broth

4 large carrots, sliced on an angle into ¼-inch pieces

1 pound small red potatoes, cut into ½-inch pieces

1 cup frozen peas

1 cup frozen corn

To make the crust: Have a deep 10-inch pie dish standing by. Line a baking sheet with parchment paper or a silicone baking mat.

In a large bowl, mix together the flour and salt. Using a pastry cutter or two forks, cut in the butter and shortening until the mixture is sandy and there are no pieces larger than a pea. Slowly add the ice water, a little at a time, gently working the mixture until the dough just comes together. You made need a bit more or less water.

Halve the dough and, on a lightly floured surface, roll out one half until it's large enough to cover the pie dish, about 16 inches in diameter. Fit the dough into the pie dish, gently pressing it into the bottom and sides. Trim the edge until it only overhangs by about ¼ inch. Fold it under to create a finished edge and gently crimp. Refrigerate until needed.

Roll the second half of dough out onto the prepared baking sheet and, using a plate that is slightly bigger than the top of your pie dish, cut a perfect circle. Find the center and create the center of the waterwheel by gently pressing a glass into the dough, creating a deep indent. Use a ruler and a pastry cutter or knife to cut the spokes, creating vents for the pie. Refrigerate the top crust until needed.

To make the filling: Preheat the oven to 425°F.

In a large, deep sauté pan over medium-high heat, heat the oil and butter until the butter foams. Add the leeks and celery and sauté until soft and beginning to brown, 4 to 5 minutes. Stir in the salt, sumac, thyme, and white pepper. Stir to combine. Sprinkle in the flour and cook, continuing to stir, for 2 minutes, or until the flour smells nutty.

continued on page 60

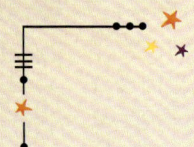

continued from page 59

Slowly add the broth and stir to incorporate, using the broth to deglaze the pan.

Add the carrots and potatoes. Simmer for 10 to 15 minutes, or until the potatoes are just tender and the broth has thickened. Remove from the heat and add the frozen peas and corn. Stir to combine.

To assemble, remove the pie dish and the top crust from the refrigerator. Fill the pie dish with the vegetable mixture and shake gently to settle. Use a second baking sheet to flip the top crust, then peel away the parchment paper and invert the crust, right-side up, onto the pie dish. Gently press the edges together. Bake for 35 to 40 minutes, or until the crust is golden brown and crisp. Allow to cool for 10 minutes, slice, and serve.

Sanderson Sisters Barbecue Fillet

The cat most definitely does *not* have Thackery's tongue when he calls Winifred Sanderson a hag. Mary suggests the boy be barbecued and filleted as punishment. It sounds extreme, but one mustn't judge her *too* harshly. No doubt scheming to suck the lives out of Salem's children has left poor Mary—and her sisters—absolutely *famished*. But the proper ingredients can bring an enterprising witch right up to speed. This savory grilled fillet practically melts in the mouth. With red and black pepper, lime juice, and a tangy chimichurri, this dish is sure to fuel a trick-or-treater—or would-be witch—all the way through Halloween night!

Yield: 4 servings | GF

For the Tri-Tip

- ½ cup red wine vinegar
- 1 tablespoon kosher salt
- Juice of 1 lime
- 6 cloves garlic, minced or pressed through a garlic press
- 1 shallot, minced
- ½ teaspoon dried oregano
- ¼ teaspoon red pepper flakes
- Fresh ground black pepper
- Stems from 1 bunch fresh cilantro (leaves reserved for chimichurri)
- Stems from 1 bunch fresh parsley (leaves reserved for chimichurri)
- 3 pounds tri-tip, trimmed of excess fat but otherwise left whole

For the Chimichurri

- 2 cloves garlic, peeled
- 1 shallot, cut into chunks
- 1 cup fresh parsley leaves
- 1 cup fresh cilantro leaves
- ¼ cup red wine vinegar
- Juice of 1 lime
- ¾ teaspoon kosher salt
- Pinch red pepper flakes
- ½ cup olive oil
- Fresh ground black pepper

To make the tri-tip: In a well-sealing container large enough to hold the piece of meat, combine the vinegar, ½ cup water, salt, lime juice, garlic, shallot, oregano, and red pepper flakes. Season with black pepper to taste. Stir to combine.

Roughly chop the cilantro and parsley stems, then add them to the marinade, stirring to combine. Add the tri-tip and turn to coat. Marinate in the refrigerator for at least 4 hours or up to 8 hours.

To barbecue the tri-tip, let the meat come to room temperature before grilling. Remove the meat from the marinade and discard the marinade.

Heat a grill to medium-high, around 400°F. Sear the meat on all sides, until well browned, about 4 minutes, then move the meat away from direct flame. Cook for 30 to 45 minutes, turning every 10 minutes and checking the internal temperature. When an instant-read thermometer inserted into the thickest part of the meat registers 135°F, remove from the grill, tent it with foil, and let it rest for at least 10 minutes before carving. You can also cook this recipe using your preferred grilling or roasting method.

To make the chimichurri: In the bowl of a food processor fitted with a blade attachment, or a blender, mince the garlic and shallot by pulsing until a fine consistency is reached. Add the parsley leaves and pulse again until most of the leaves are minced. Add the cilantro leaves and pulse again until everything is minced.

Add the vinegar, lime juice, salt, and red pepper flakes, then pulse again several times to combine. With the motor running, slowly add the olive oil until it is all incorporated. Season with black pepper to taste. Transfer to an airtight container and refrigerate until about 30 minutes before serving.

Allow to come to room temperature, then serve with the tri-tip.

Main Dishes

Cheese Puff Chicken Tenders

Mary makes herself *quite* at home in Master's house. She curls up in his favorite easy chair and happily stuffs her face with a bowl of cheese puffs she finds on the table. Although Master's wife is unimpressed—and in fact, develops an immediate loathing for the snack-happy witch— these cheesy, crunchy chicken tenders will be beloved by young and old alike. The littlest witches may enjoy them plain, while those with more adventurous palates might serve them over salad… or with a side of Dead Man's Toes (page 25)! However one prefers them, these chicken tenders are a staple in any Salem household. No witchcraft necessary!

Yield: 6 servings | GF*

For the Sauce
- ¾ cup sour cream
- ¼ cup mayonnaise
- 1 tablespoon mustard
- ½ teaspoon onion powder
- ¼ teaspoon salt
- Fresh ground black pepper
- Dash hot sauce (optional)

For the Chicken Tenders
- 2 cups buttermilk
- ½ teaspoon kosher salt
- ½ teaspoon paprika
- ¼ teaspoon onion powder
- 1 tablespoon mustard
- 4 pounds chicken breast tenderloins
- 14 ounces cheese puffs, pulverized

Note
This recipe can be easily made gluten-free by using a gluten-free cheese puff.

To make the sauce: In a small bowl, combine the sour cream, mayonnaise, mustard, onion powder, and salt. Season with black pepper to taste and add hot sauce (if using). Mix well and refrigerate until serving.

To make the chicken tenders: In a large container that seals well, combine the buttermilk, salt, paprika, onion powder, and mustard. Add the chicken and turn until well coated. Refrigerate for 30 minutes.

Preheat the oven and two baking sheets to 425°F. Line a third baking sheet with parchment paper.

Set up a dredging station by covering a large plate with about a third of the cheese puffs. One at a time, remove the chicken tenders from the marinade and dredge in the cheese puff coating, pressing gently to help it adhere. Place the coated tender on the third prepared baking sheet. When the parchment paper is full, carefully transfer the chicken on its parchment to one of the baking sheets in the oven. Line the third baking sheet with another piece of parchment. Repeat this process, adding more cheese puff coating to the plate as needed, until all the tenders are coated and in the oven.

Bake for 15 to 18 minutes, or until crisp and golden brown and an instant-read thermometer inserted into the thickest part of the chicken registers 165°F.

Allow to rest on the baking sheets for 2 to 3 minutes, then serve with the sauce on the side.

Main Dishes

Hollywood Barbecue Chicken Pizza

When the graveyard bullies find out Max is from California, they immediately give him a snarky nickname: Hollywood. But even these bullies would have nothing but praise for Hollywood's protein-packed signature dish. A tasty twist on a popular party favorite, this chicken pizza blends the traditional doughy base with a fiery barbecued topping. Tangy, savory, and quintessentially Californian, this slice of Hollywood is sure to please any hungry high schooler—or a trio of kindly old spinster ladies!

Yield: 2 pizzas or about 6 servings | GF*

For the Pizza Sauce
- 1 tablespoon olive oil
- 1 tablespoon balsamic vinegar
- One 28-ounce can crushed tomatoes
- 1 teaspoon salt
- ½ teaspoon dried oregano
- Fresh ground black pepper

For the Barbecue Sauce
- ¼ cup apple cider vinegar
- 2 tablespoons dark brown sugar
- 1 teaspoon salt
- ½ teaspoon ground cayenne
- ½ teaspoon onion powder
- One 15-ounce can tomato sauce
- ¼ cup molasses

For the Pizza
- Two 14-ounce store-bought pizza doughs
- 4 cups shredded mozzarella, divided
- 1½ pounds grilled boneless skinless chicken thighs or precooked chicken, shredded, divided
- 1 cup shredded cheddar, divided
- ½ red onion, thinly sliced, divided
- 4 green onions, white and light green parts only, thinly sliced, divided

To make the pizza sauce: In a medium saucepan over medium-high heat, combine the olive oil, balsamic vinegar, and crushed tomatoes. Add the salt and oregano and season with black pepper to taste. Bring to a rolling boil, then turn the heat to low and simmer until the sauce is reduced by a third, 20 to 30 minutes.

To make the barbecue sauce: While the pizza sauce simmers, in a medium saucepan over medium heat, combine the apple cider vinegar, brown sugar, salt, cayenne, and onion powder and stir. Add the tomato sauce and molasses, stirring to combine. Bring to a simmer, then turn the heat to low and continue to simmer until the sauce reduces by a third, about 20 minutes.

To make the pizza: Preheat the oven and two baking sheets to 425°F.

On a lightly oiled piece of parchment paper big enough to cover the baking sheet, roll or stretch out one piece of the dough into a rough rectangle. Spread 1 cup of the pizza sauce over the dough and top with half of the mozzarella. Scatter half of the chicken over the cheese and drizzle with ½ cup of the barbecue sauce. Scatter half of the cheddar, half of the red onion, and half of the green onion over that. Repeat the process with the second piece of dough and the remaining ingredients.

Use an extra baking sheet or large cutting board to transfer the pizza on its parchment paper to the oven. Gently slide the parchment and pizza onto the preheated baking sheets. Bake, rotating halfway through, for 10 to 12 minutes, or until the cheese is bubbly and the crust is golden brown.

Notes
Leftover Roasted Red Spice Chicken (page 49) works well for the chicken in this dish.

This recipe can be easily made gluten-free by using gluten-free or cauliflower pizza crusts.

Main Dishes

Tie-Dye California Smoothie Bowl

There's a lot to be said for the Californian laid-back, tie-dyed point of view. Those who embrace it have been known to be less stressed, holistically balanced, and uncompromisingly health-conscious. This fruit-filled smoothie bowl summons the spirit of a signature snack from Max's home state. With Greek yogurt, raspberries, and blue spirulina, it's sure to make even a Hollywood expat feel right at home.

Yield: 2 smoothie bowls | GF*, V, V+*

1 cup Greek yogurt

2 teaspoons honey

½ teaspoon blue spirulina powder

½ cup frozen raspberries

½ cup coconut water, divided

½ cup frozen mangoes

½ cup granola, divided

1 cup fresh raspberries

1 cup fresh blueberries, plus more for garnish

2 tablespoons chia seeds

In a small bowl, combine the yogurt, honey, and blue spirulina. Refrigerate.

In a small blender, combine the frozen raspberries with ¼ cup of the coconut water and puree. Transfer to a small pitcher or measuring cup and refrigerate. Starting with a clean blender, puree the remaining ¼ cup of coconut water and the mango, then refrigerate.

Evenly divide the granola between two large, shallow bowls. Top with the fresh raspberries and blueberries. Divide the yogurt evenly between the two bowls, carefully spreading it out to reach the rim of the bowl.

Pour or spoon the raspberry puree into the middle of each bowl, being careful to leave a border of yogurt. Repeat with the mango puree, placing it in the center of the raspberry. Use a knife to drag through the colors, creating a fun pattern (or you can let your guests create their own).

Decorate with more blueberries around the edge, if desired, and sprinkle the chia seeds to create a peace symbol in the center.

Note

This recipe can be easily made gluten-free by choosing your favorite gluten-free granola, and vegan by using a plant-based yogurt.

Desserts

Long ago, All Hallows' Eve was celebrated as the night when souls of the dead could return to earth. Nowadays, similarly named Halloween is a night when children dress in costumes and consume copious amounts of sweets. The desserts within these pages were created in honor of that sugar-filled night—and they're sure to put an otherworldly spell on you! From Winnie's Magical Popping Candy (page 86)—a mischievous meal in itself!—to Black River Brownie Bars (page 87)—thankfully, 'tis not too firm!—these recipes offer a magical medley of gastronomic delights.

Thackery Binx Treats

In his life as a cat, Binx has spent years hunting mice down in the old Salem Crypt. After all, one does what one must to survive a Sanderson curse! But there's nothing cursed about these Binx-inspired treats. Perfectly sweetened cherries are dipped in chocolate and topped with almonds to create the most adorable critters that Salem's ever seen. As Dani might say, hunting mice just got a lot more fun!

Yield: 12 to 16 mice | GF, V

One 13-ounce jar natural bar cherries, stem on and pitted

About ¼ cup sliced almonds

16 wrapped chocolate kiss-shaped candies

1 cup semisweet chocolate chips

1 tablespoon shortening

Small nonpareils for making eyes

Pour the jar of cherries and their juices into a large bowl. Sort through and find 12 to 16 cherries with nice long stems and good shapes, not crushed or broken. Return the rest of the cherries and their syrup to the jar and reserve for future use.

Rinse the selected cherries in a fine-mesh strainer and turn out onto paper towels to thoroughly dry.

While the cherries are drying, line a baking sheet with parchment paper or a silicone baking mat. Sort the almonds and create pairs of ears and unwrap enough chocolate candies for each cherry.

Melt the chocolate chips in a chocolate melting pot or a small microwave-safe bowl in 30-second bursts, heating as few times as possible and stirring to complete the melting. Stir in the shortening until the mixture is smooth.

Dip each cherry, holding on to the stem, into the chocolate and make sure it covers all the way to the stem. Shake off excess chocolate and then press the bottom of the cherry to the flat side of the kiss. Lay the pair down on its side, with the stem at one end and the point of the kiss at the other. Press two almond slices into the chocolate just behind the kiss, creating the ears. Continue until all the cherries have been dipped.

continued on page 72

continued from page 70

Using a toothpick or skewer, dot each kiss right in front of the ears with two dots of chocolate and stick the nonpareils on to make eyes. Allow to set for 10 to 15 minutes at room temperature or for 5 minutes in the refrigerator.

Serve immediately or store carefully between layers of parchment paper in an airtight container for up to three days.

"Hey, Cupcake" Cupcakes

Be careful what you wish for! When an enthusiastic bus driver greets Sarah with an appreciative, "Hey, cupcake," he thinks he's greeting a gorgeous creature—one he very much hopes he'll be seeing again. These vanilla cupcakes offer a happy nod to that unwitting driver. With brown butter buttercream and crushed butterscotch candies, these cupcakes have been known to disappear lickety-split. In no time at all, you'll be bidding farewell to the entire batch . . . *and* a certain "mortal bus boy"!

Yield: About 24 cupcakes | V

For the Cupcakes

- 2 cups all-purpose flour
- 2 teaspoons baking powder
- ½ teaspoon salt
- 2 cups sugar
- 16 tablespoons (2 sticks) unsalted butter, softened
- 6 large eggs
- 2 tablespoons vanilla extract

For the Frosting and Tuile Garnish

- 16 tablespoons (2 sticks) unsalted butter, cut into small pieces
- 1 teaspoon kosher salt
- 1 tablespoon vanilla extract
- 6 cups powdered sugar
- ⅓ cup heavy cream
- 12 unwrapped butterscotch candies (optional)

Specialty Tools

Pastry bag and large star tips (optional)

To make the cupcakes: Preheat the oven to 350°F and line two muffin pans with liners.

In a medium bowl, whisk together the flour, baking powder, and salt and set aside.

In the bowl of a stand mixer fitted with the paddle attachment, cream together the sugar and butter on medium speed until light and fluffy, about 3 minutes. Add the eggs, one at a time, beating well after each addition to keep the mixture light and fluffy. With the final egg, add the vanilla.

Working in two batches, fold in the flour mixture, scraping down the bowl as you go. Fill each muffin liner two-thirds full. Bake for 20 to 25 minutes, or until a cake tester inserted into the center comes out clean. Rotate the pans halfway through baking. Allow to cool in the pan for 10 minutes, then transfer the cupcakes to a wire rack to cool completely before frosting.

To make the frosting and garnish: In a large heavy-bottomed saucepan over medium heat, heat the butter, stirring, until completely melted. Continue stirring until the butter clarifies and begins to brown. The butter will foam and bubble, but continue stirring. When the butter has reached a deep golden brown and has a nutty scent, 5 to 7 minutes total, remove from the heat. Decant to a large bowl and allow to cool completely.

Add the salt and vanilla and stir to combine. Add the powdered sugar, 1 cup at a time, beating with a hand mixer on medium-high speed after each addition. The mixture will eventually become stiff and crumbly.

continued on page 74

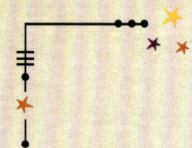

continued from page 73

Continue beating while slowly adding in the heavy cream until the mixture has reached a smooth consistency. Note that you may need 1 tablespoon less or 1 tablespoon more of heavy cream to achieve an easily spreadable consistency.

Frost each cupcake with an offset spatula or a pastry bag fitted with a large star tip.

Start the butterscotch tuile garnish (if using) by preheating the oven to 350°F.

On a baking sheet lined with a silicone baking mat, place the butterscotch candies at least 2 inches apart.

Bake for 8 minutes, or until just starting to spread. Place a piece of parchment paper over the candies and press down with a heavy glass or jar. Twist gently to create the sheer edges. Allow to cool completely. Remove the parchment, break each candy in half, and store in between pieces of parchment paper in an airtight container until needed. Don't worry if they don't break perfectly in half; the organic shapes and shards are what make this a fun garnish.

Top the cupcakes with the tuiles and serve.

Winnie's Spellbook Cake

Winifred Sanderson's beloved book was given to her by Master himself. Its contents are said to contain her "most powerful and evil spells," and it's feared throughout the community of Salem. Although this dessert requires no dark magic, its dark chocolate base and buttercream filling make it a flavorful favorite. Just be sure to keep it away from magic candles—black flame or otherwise!

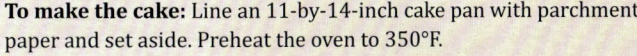

Yield: 12 to 14 servings | V

For the Cake

- 8 tablespoons (1 stick) unsalted butter
- ¾ cup light brown sugar
- ¾ cup granulated sugar
- 2 large eggs
- 2 teaspoons vanilla extract
- 1 cup cocoa powder
- 1½ cups all-purpose flour
- 2 teaspoons baking powder
- ¼ teaspoon salt
- ⅔ cup sour cream
- 1 cup hot water

continued on page 78

To make the cake: Line an 11-by-14-inch cake pan with parchment paper and set aside. Preheat the oven to 350°F.

In the bowl of a stand mixer fitted with the paddle attachment, cream together the butter and both sugars on medium-high speed until light and fluffy, about 3 minutes. Add the eggs and vanilla. Beat again until well combined. Add the cocoa powder and mix again until completely incorporated.

In a small bowl, mix together the flour, baking powder, and salt.

Add half of the flour mixture to the butter mixture and mix until incorporated. Scrape down the sides of the bowl and add the sour cream all at once. Mix until completely incorporated. Add the remaining flour mixture, mix again, and scrape down the sides of the bowl.

With the mixer running on low speed, slowly drizzle in the hot water. Continue to mix until all of the water is incorporated and batter is smooth, 2 to 3 minutes.

Pour the batter into the prepared cake pan and bake for 25 to 30 minutes, or until a cake tester inserted into the center comes out clean. Allow to cool in the pan for 15 minutes before inverting onto a wire rack and removing the parchment. Allow to cool completely.

continued on page 78

Desserts

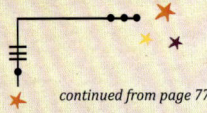

continued from page 77

For the Filling and Frosting

6 egg whites

¼ teaspoon salt

2 cups dark brown sugar

1 teaspoon fresh lemon juice

3 cups (6 sticks) unsalted butter, cut into tablespoons, plus more for greasing

2 teaspoons vanilla extract

6 ounces semisweet chocolate, melted

1 cup crushed chocolate wafer cookies (optional)

About 30 chocolate chew candies

About 2 teaspoons silver luster dust

¼ teaspoon gold or bronze luster dust

About 1 tablespoon black cocoa, cocoa, or black petal dust

Specialty Tools

Candy thermometer

continued from page 77

To make the filling and frosting: Add the egg whites and salt to the bowl of a stand mixer fitted with a whisk attachment. In a medium heavy-bottomed saucepan over medium-high heat, combine the brown sugar with 1 cup of water and bring to a boil. Set the mixer on medium speed and whisk until the eggs are frothy, about 1 minute. Add the lemon juice and whisk until soft peaks form, 2 to 3 minutes more, then shut off the mixer.

Grease a heatproof 4-cup measuring cup with butter and set aside. Fit the saucepan with a candy thermometer and, when the sugar mixture reaches 238°F, decant it to the measuring cup.

Slowly add the sugar syrup to the egg whites in small batches, whisking after each addition. When all the syrup is added, beat the mixture on high speed until the meringue is completely cool (the outside of the bowl should be cool to the touch), 3 to 5 minutes.

Add the butter, one to two pieces at a time, beating well on medium speed after each addition. Once all the butter has been incorporated, add the vanilla and briefly beat on high speed until smooth.

Reserve 4 cups of the frosting to fill the cake and create the pages and add the melted chocolate to the rest. Beat again until smooth, about 1 minute.

To assemble the cake: Cut the cake exactly down the middle horizontally, creating 2 smaller layer cakes of equal size. Place one layer onto your desired cake or serving board. Use 2 cups of the plain frosting to fill the cake by frosting a thick layer onto this cake layer with an offset spatula. If using, sprinkle the crushed cookies on top of the frosting. Top with the second cake layer and use the offset spatula to "seal" the edges by pushing frosting into the space. Chill in the refrigerator as is for 10 minutes.

Remove from the refrigerator and frost the top of the cake and the back edge (this will become the spine of the book) with the chocolate frosting. Use the offset spatula to create neat edges along the front and sides of the cake to create the book cover. Reserve about ½ cup of the chocolate frosting, storing in an airtight container at room temperature. You will need this to attach the embellishments. Chill again for 15 to 20 minutes.

Remove from the refrigerator and use the remaining 2 cups of plain frosting to pipe the exposed front and side edges, creating the pages. Be careful not to touch the "book cover." Chill again for 10 minutes, or more, before using a long knife or metal ruler to "cut" pages into the edges. As straight as possible, firmly press the edge of the knife or ruler into the frosting, over and over, until you have created lines

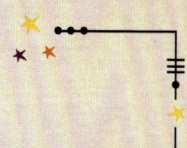

representing the pages from top to bottom. Repeat on the sides, lining up the lines as best you can. Keep in mind the spellbook is a very old book, so imperfections just make it more realistic. Return the cake to the refrigerator while you create the embellishments.

You will need a nonstick surface such as a silicone baking mat or parchment paper, wooden skewers, and a microwave-safe plate. Place 3 unwrapped chocolate chews on the plate and microwave 5 to 10 seconds, until just pliable. Knead together until they are 1 smooth ball. Roll out the ball on the nonstick surface until you have a 12- to 13-inch snake, making sure to thin out one end for the tail. Gently pinch and flatten the other end to create the head. Coil the snake and set aside. Repeat for one more coiled snake and then make one snake for the top of the spine. Measure the length of your frosted cake to make sure it will fit.

Use about 1½ candy chews each, again gently heated, to create 5 fingers for the book spine, using the skewer to create details such as nails and knuckles. Gently heat another 6 candies, knead them together, and roll them out to about ⅛ inch thick. From this, cut the rounded triangles that sit under the coiled snakes, and the straight strip that sits under the third snake. Use 5 candies to sculpt the lock pieces. For the base of the stitches, use another 2 candies and roll them out to thin ropes of varying lengths, fold each rope in half, creating a double strand, and then gently flatten it.

Use the silver luster dust and a small, clean brush to "paint" the snakes, snake bases, and lock pieces. Age the pieces with the black cocoa or black petal dust. Age the fingers with the cocoa as well.

Remove the cake from the refrigerator and use little dabs of the reserved frosting to attach all the embellishments. Do the stitches last, fitting them in around the other decor as desired. Place the remaining frosting in a disposable pastry bag, snip a small hole in the tip, and pipe the stitches, then pipe perpendicularly over the base stitch lines. For the final step, use the black cocoa to age the rest of the book and pages by gently dusting it on with a pastry brush.

The cake can be made up to a week ahead, wrapped, and frozen. Do not defrost before decorating. The decorated cake can be made a day ahead and should be kept in the refrigerator until about 45 minutes before serving.

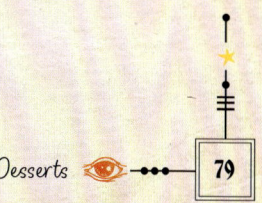

Classic Caramel Apple Dip

Bobbing for apples is a time-honored tradition. And this tangy twist on a sweet classic will have Halloween revelers bouncing with excitement. A light, creamy whip offers a delightful dipping sauce for thin apple slices—and their bat, cat, or ghost cutouts! Packed with vitamins (and just a sprinkle of sugar), this appley snack is sure to be the hit of any party—no bobbing required!

Yield: 8 servings | GF, V

- 8 ounces cream cheese, softened
- ¼ cup Greek yogurt
- ¼ cup dark brown sugar
- ½ tablespoon vanilla extract
- 4 large apples
- 1 tablespoon apple cider vinegar, plus more as needed (optional)
- Sliced almonds (optional)

Specialty Tools
Small Halloween cookie cutters, such as bats, cats, and ghosts (optional)

In a medium bowl using a hand mixer on medium speed, combine the cream cheese and yogurt until light and fluffy. Add the brown sugar and beat until completely incorporated. Add the vanilla and mix again. Store in an airtight container in the refrigerator until ready to serve.

The apples can be prepared a few ways:

1. Quarter, core, and slice apples into wedges. Toss all cut apples with the apple cider vinegar to coat them. Serve alongside the dip.

2. Slice the apples from end to end into thin rounds and use the cookie cutters to core and make fun shapes. Serve alongside the dip.

3. Quarter, core, and slice the apples into wedges. Use two wedges to create a monster mouth. Spread about 2 teaspoons of the dip onto one slice of apple and top with a second slice, making sure the peel sides are facing the same way. Insert almond slices as fangs and serve.

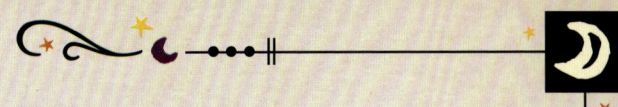

Broomstick, and Other Transport, Treats

Common household cleaning tools are the Sanderson sisters' preferred means of travel. But after three hundred years, many things have changed—and not always for the better. While Winnie and Sarah are able to fly into the night on a trusty old broomstick and mop, respectively, poor Mary must make do with a thoroughly modern vacuum. But no matter the vehicle, each of these enchanting broomstick treats is filled with peanut butter cups and molded to resemble one of the Sanderson sisters' trusty old (or new!) rides. Into the night!

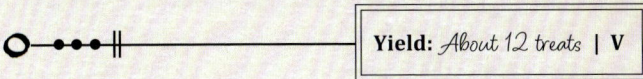

Yield: About 12 treats | V

For the Cake

4 tablespoons unsalted butter
¾ cup light brown sugar
1 large egg
1 teaspoon vanilla extract
½ cup cocoa powder
¾ cup all-purpose flour
1 teaspoon baking powder
⅛ teaspoon salt
⅓ cup smooth peanut butter
½ cup hot water

continued on page 84

Line an 8-by-8-inch baking pan with parchment paper and set aside. Preheat the oven to 350°F.

To make the cake: In a large bowl using a hand mixer on medium speed, cream together the butter and brown sugar until light and fluffy, about 3 minutes. Add the egg and vanilla and beat again until well combined. Add the cocoa powder and mix again until completely incorporated.

In a small bowl, mix together the flour, baking powder, and salt.

Add half of the flour mixture to the butter mixture and mix again until incorporated. Scrape down the sides of the bowl and add the peanut butter all at once. Mix until completely incorporated. Add the remaining flour mixture, mix again, and scrape down the sides of the bowl.

With the mixer on low speed, slowly drizzle in the hot water. Continue to mix until all of the water is incorporated and the batter is smooth, 2 to 3 minutes.

Pour the batter into the prepared pan and bake for 10 to 15 minutes, or until a cake tester inserted into the center comes out clean. Allow to cool in the pan for 30 minutes, then break the cake up and transfer it to a large bowl. Refrigerate until completely cool, at least 1 hour.

continued on page 84

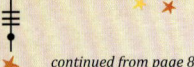

continued from page 83

For the Frosting

8 tablespoons (1 stick) unsalted butter, softened

⅔ cup powdered sugar

⅓ cup cocoa powder

1 teaspoon vanilla extract

2 tablespoons heavy cream

For Assembly

12 to 14 pretzel rods

8 unwrapped thin peanut butter cups (dark chocolate is a nice touch here)

20 ounces dark melting chocolate

5 ounces white melting chocolate

1 to 2 drops bright-green food coloring

24 inches black licorice lace (optional)

3 ounces peanut butter baking chips

continued from page 83

To make the frosting: In a large bowl using a hand mixer on low speed, mix together the butter, powdered sugar, and cocoa powder until well combined but still crumbly. Add the vanilla and heavy cream. Continue to mix on medium speed until light and fluffy, about 2 minutes.

Add the frosting to the cake crumbles and use the mixer on low speed to combine until a dough forms.

To assemble: Line a baking sheet with a silicone baking mat. Assemble the pretzel rods and the unwrapped peanut butter cups on the sheet. Halve four of the peanut butter cups and set aside.

Working with about 3 tablespoons of cake dough, use your hands to form it into a broom shape around the end of a pretzel rod. Press the base of the "broom" over a peanut butter cup half, covering it partly with the cake dough and creating a firm, stable base. Lay the broom down on the baking sheet and continue until you have four brooms. Reserve the remaining peanut butter cup halves.

Again working with about 3 tablespoons of cake dough, form a round "mop" shape around one end of a pretzel rod. Press the bottom of the mop over a whole peanut butter cup, partially covering it with dough and creating a firm base. Lay the mop down on the baking sheet and continue until you have four mops.

To make the vacuums, break two pretzel sticks roughly in half (don't worry, you have a few extra) and use 3 tablespoons of dough to form a vacuum shape on the broken end of a pretzel stick. Use a reserved peanut butter cup half to create a firm base, rounded edge facing front, by pressing the cake pop gently over the cup and using the shape to help form the front of the vacuum. Leave the vacuums standing up on the tray.

Freeze all the cake pops for 1 hour.

When the hour is almost up, melt the dark chocolate in a chocolate melting pot or medium microwave-safe bowl in 30-second bursts. Remove the cake pops from the freezer. Dip each cake pop into the melted chocolate, making sure to coat the joint between cake and pretzel rod. You may need a small spatula to help cover the whole cake pop. Gently shake off excess chocolate and set it, base-side down, standing up on the baking sheet. Repeat until you have covered all the cake pops.

Next, using a clean melting pot or small microwave-safe bowl in 30-second bursts, melt the white chocolate. Using a pastry brush (a silicone one works best for this job), brush the "mop" bases with streaks of white chocolate to create the strings of the mops. Repeat with all four mops, setting them back on the baking sheet as you go.

Once all the mops have been decorated, take a small amount of leftover white chocolate, about 1 tablespoon, and dye it green with the green food coloring. Use a small spatula or demitasse spoon to decorate the front of the vacuum with the green white chocolate. Use a small dot of the green chocolate to adhere a 6-inch piece of licorice (if using) to the back as the cord.

Using the remaining white chocolate as a base, add the peanut butter chips and melt in the microwave in 30-second bursts, stirring until combined and smooth. Use a clean pastry brush (again silicone is best in this case) to brush on the broom bristles. Refrigerate all the cake pops for 5 to 7 minutes, or until all the chocolate is set.

The cake pops can be stored in an airtight container between layers of parchment paper for up to four days. They can also be wrapped in cellophane bags and gifted as favors.

Winnie's Magical Popping Candy

Winifred Sanderson has countless spells up her sleeve. She can turn a boy into a cat . . . or eke the youth from an unsuspecting child. And she's been known to put on quite the show by using her magic to create all kinds of fantastical explosions! With shocking bursts of sweetness, this popping candy conjures up the spirit of a firecracker of a witch. It's destined to be a true crowd-pleaser—one that's absolutely bubbling with flavor!

Yield: 2 cups | GF, V, V+

1½ tablespoons citric acid, divided

1 teaspoon baking soda (see note)

1 cup sugar

2 tablespoons corn syrup

½ teaspoon kosher salt

2 to 3 drops bright-green food coloring

¼ teaspoon orange extract

Specialty Tools
Candy thermometer

Note
Make sure your baking soda is active and not expired.

Line a rimmed baking sheet with parchment paper and sprinkle ½ tablespoon of the citric acid over it. Set aside. In a small bowl, mix together the baking soda and remaining 1 tablespoon of citric acid and set aside.

In a medium heavy-bottomed saucepan, carefully pour the sugar into the center of the pan. Pour 2 tablespoons water and the corn syrup around the edge. Place the pan over medium heat and use a wooden spoon to gently pull the moisture through the sugar. Once all the sugar is moistened, clip a candy thermometer to the side of the pan and let the mixture boil without stirring until it reaches 300°F.

Remove from the heat, add the baking soda mixture all at once, and stir. Be careful as the mixture will bubble and foam! Keep stirring until all the powder has been incorporated. Add the food coloring and orange extract and stir until even in color. Pour out onto the prepared baking sheet, and spread into an even layer. You will not necessarily cover the whole sheet. Allow to cool completely and then immediately break into small chunks and store in an airtight container for up to one week.

Black River Brownie Bars

The Sanderson sisters haven't been around for the past three hundred years. In that time, the world has witnessed many advances—cars, buses, and the roads necessary to convey gorgeous creatures, such as the sisters, from here to there. But while those roads may look a fair bit like a black river, their namesake brownies are far from firm as stone. With black cocoa, semisweet chocolate chips, and a black river cream cheese swirl, these brownie bars are a mouthwatering treat!

Yield: About 12 bars | V

4 ounces unsweetened baking chocolate, broken into small pieces

12 tablespoons (1½ sticks) salted butter

1¼ cups granulated sugar, divided

1 cup dark brown sugar

4 large eggs, divided

1½ teaspoons vanilla extract, divided

1 cup all-purpose flour

1 cup semisweet chocolate chips

3 tablespoons black cocoa powder (see note)

8 ounces cream cheese, softened

Notes

Black cocoa powder is available online and in specialty stores. It will give your brownies an extra dark color and unique depth of flavor. However, regular cocoa powder can be substituted.

For the cleanest cuts, chill the brownies in the pan in the refrigerator for about 30 minutes.

Preheat the oven to 350°F.

Line a 9-by-11-inch baking pan with parchment paper so that the paper hangs over the ends.

In a large microwave-safe bowl, combine the baking chocolate and butter. Microwave for 1 minute and stir to completely melt chocolate and butter. If needed, microwave 30 seconds more. Add 1 cup of the granulated sugar and the brown sugar, stirring to combine.

Add three of the eggs, one at a time, stirring briskly after each addition. Add 1 teaspoon of the vanilla, stirring to combine. Add the flour and stir to completely combine.

Remove about ½ cup from the batter and set aside. Mix the chocolate chips into the remaining portion of brownie batter, then spread the mixture evenly on the bottom of the prepared baking pan.

In a clean medium bowl, use a hand mixer on medium speed to beat the cream cheese, remaining ¼ cup of sugar, remaining ½ teaspoon of vanilla, remaining 1 egg, and the black cocoa until light and fluffy, 1 to 2 minutes.

Spread the cream cheese mixture over the brownie mixture. Dot the cream cheese mixture with the remaining brownie mixture and use a knife to swirl. Bake for 35 to 40 minutes, or until a cake tester inserted into the center comes out fudgy but not wet.

Allow to cool completely before cutting and serving. Store in an airtight container for up to three days.

Desserts

Witch Cookie Pops

The sisters three are somewhat fair,
With warty skin and wild hair.
But come the morning they'll reclaim
Their youth and looks—in Master's name.
This witchy pop will bring them glee—

Their likeness on a grand cookie!
'Twas loved by Dani when she tried
A pop while at Allison's side.
So make a batch. Look to the sky
Where broomsticks soar. "Sisters! We fly!"

Yield: *About 16 cookie pops* | **V**

For the Cookies

12 tablespoons (1½ sticks) salted butter, softened

4 ounces cream cheese, softened

¾ cup sugar

½ cup cocoa powder

1 teaspoon vanilla extract

1 large egg

2½ cups all-purpose flour

For the Royal Icing

4 cups powdered sugar, sifted

3 tablespoons meringue powder

1 to 2 drops black, green, purple, yellow, and/or orange food coloring

Specialty Tools

Halloween cookie cutters

Sixteen 6-inch paper lollipop sticks

Pastry bags and writing tips

To make the cookies: In a large bowl using a hand mixer or the bowl of a stand mixer fitted with the paddle attachment, beat the butter on medium-high speed until light and fluffy, 1 to 2 minutes. Add the cream cheese and beat again until the mixture is smooth, fluffy, and pale. Add the sugar and mix until completely incorporated. Add the cocoa powder and vanilla and mix again until completely incorporated. Add the egg and mix again. Add the flour in two batches, mixing after each addition, until completely incorporated.

Split the dough into two pieces, flatten into disks, wrap in parchment paper, and chill in the refrigerator for at least 1 hour.

Working with one disk at a time, roll out the dough to about ⅛ inch thick on a lightly floured silicone baking mat (see note). Using Halloween cookie cutters, cut out the desired shapes and peel off the excess dough. Rewrap and chill scraps to roll out more cookies.

Using an offset spatula, gently lift the bottom half of each cookie and place a lollipop stick under it. Make sure the stick has lots of cookie coverage, at least 2 inches, even if it needs to be at an angle for some shapes. Set the cookie back down onto the stick and use your fingers to gently press the dough onto the stick. Slide the baking mat onto a baking sheet and chill in the refrigerator for 15 minutes before baking.

While the cookies are chilling, preheat the oven to 350°F. Roll out more dough on another baking mat and cut out more cookies, repeating the steps above. Chill each batch for at least 15 minutes before baking.

When the cookies have chilled, bake them for 9 to 11 minutes, or until firm in the middle and starting to barely crisp around the edges. Allow to cool on the baking mat on a wire rack.

continued on page 90

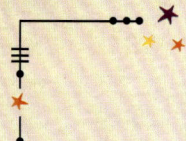

continued from page 89

To make the icing: In the bowl of a stand mixer fitted with the whisk attachment, combine the powdered sugar, meringue powder, and 6 tablespoons water. Whisk on low speed for 7 to 10 minutes, or until the icing holds stiff peaks. (If using a hand mixer, whisk on high speed for 10 to 12 minutes.) Divide the icing into small bowls and use the food coloring to create your desired colors. Transfer the icing to pastry bags fitted with writing tips.

To decorate, turn each cookie over, exposing the lollipop stick, and pipe a thin stripe of icing in your desired color over the stick. Allow to dry for 30 to 40 minutes before turning over and decorating as desired. Allow the cookies to dry completely before serving, packaging, or storing, at least 3 hours. Store in an airtight container between layers of parchment paper or place each cookie in a cellophane bag for gifting.

Notes

Rolling out your cookies directly on the baking mat means you won't need to move delicate shapes. Just lift away the excess dough, leaving behind your cutouts.

While black icing is a go-to choice for Halloween, it can also stain fabrics. If serving cookies to small children, you may want to let the chocolate dough stand in for the black icing or use other creative colors! After all, the Sanderson sisters never wear basic black! Black icing can also temporarily stain tongues and lips, but this can add to the Halloween fun!

Desserts | 91

Dad-cula Fang Strawberries

Only the coolest dads can pull off a *dad*-cula vampire costume. But *anyone* can whip up these treats, which are inspired by the truly incomparable Mr. Dennison. Fresh strawberries pair gloriously with a semisweet chocolate filling and white chocolate coating, yielding a succulently sweet creation that's sure to have dads, moms, and children alike dancing with joy.

Yield: *About 24 fangs* | GF, V

Ingredients:
- 1 pound strawberries, rinsed and hulled
- 2 tablespoons heavy cream
- ½ cup semisweet chocolate chips
- About 15 ounces white chocolate melting wafers

Dry the strawberries well. Have a mini muffin pan standing by.

In a medium microwave-safe bowl, pour the heavy cream over the chocolate chips. Microwave in 30-second bursts for 1 minute, let the ganache stand for 3 minutes, then stir until well melted.

Using a small spoon, fill each strawberry cavity with ganache and rest in a mini muffin cavity. Once all the strawberries have been filled with ganache, put the mini muffin pan in the refrigerator for 15 minutes to set.

Line a baking sheet with parchment paper and keep it close by. In a separate small microwave-safe bowl, melt the white chocolate in 30-second bursts two to three times, stirring after each time, until completely smooth.

Dip each strawberry, chocolate-filled-side down, leaving the tip of each strawberry exposed. Work quickly so as not to melt the chocolate. Shake off excess chocolate and place the strawberry on the prepared baking sheet. Once all the strawberries have been coated, refrigerate for 5 minutes to set.

Serve immediately or store in an airtight container between layers of parchment paper for up to 24 hours.

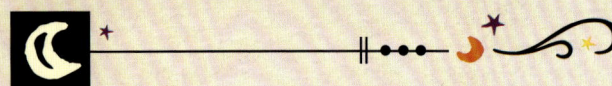

Twisted Winifred Spirals

Winifred Sanderson's towering crimson buns that playfully sit atop her head lend an air of mischief to her formidable persona. Just like the witchy sister herself, these spirals combine a dash of sweetness with a dose of spice. Cinnamon, cayenne, and a few spoonfuls of sugar melt into a buttery puff pastry to create the ultimate mini palmier—no spells required!

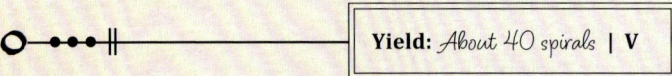

Yield: *About 40 spirals* | V

1 cup finely chopped pecans, toasted (see note)

½ cup sugar

1 tablespoon ground cinnamon

¼ teaspoon ground cayenne

One 17-ounce box puff pastry, thawed according to package directions

2 tablespoons salted butter, melted

Red sanding sugar for decorating (optional)

Note

To toast nuts, heat a small stainless-steel or cast-iron pan on the stove over medium-high heat for about 1 minute. Add the nuts, stir, and then remove the pan from the heat. Continue to stir the nuts until fragrant, about 2 minutes.

In a small bowl, combine the cooled toasted nuts with the sugar, cinnamon, and cayenne and set aside.

Roll out each piece of puff pastry on a lightly floured surface into a 12-by-12-inch square.

On a large piece of parchment paper or silicone baking mat, sprinkle about ½ cup of the nut mixture on the surface, covering approximately a 12-by-12-inch space. Cover the mixture with one of the pastry squares. Roll over the square with a rolling pin to press the pastry into the nut mixture. Brush the top of the pastry piece with half of the melted butter and scatter another ½ cup of the nut mixture onto the top of the pastry, spreading out evenly and to the edges. Roll the rolling pin over the top one more time to press the nut mixture into the dough.

Fold each side toward the middle so the two edges meet dead center, gather nut mixture from underneath, and press it into any blank parts of the pastry. Fold each side in half again and then fold the entire piece in half at the center seam. You should have a long rectangle made of eight layers of pastry. Some nut mixture may be left behind; use this for the next piece. Place the dough on a baking sheet and place it in the freezer for 15 minutes. Repeat with the second piece of pastry.

While the pastry is chilling, preheat the oven to 400°F. Line a baking sheet with parchment paper or a silicone baking mat.

Remove the pastry from the freezer and slice into ¼-inch-thick slices. Place them on the prepared baking sheet, spaced 1 inch apart. Sprinkle with red sanding sugar (if using) and bake for 12 to 15 minutes, or until golden brown and crisp.

Allow to cool on the baking sheet and then serve or store in an airtight container for up to three days.

Puffed Rice Potion Bottles

Some potions steal youth. Some strip children of their baby fat. And others exist for the sole purpose of bringing lots and lots of happiness. These blue and green potion bottles cheerfully camp in the happiness category. With rich butter, fluffy marshmallows, and a sprinkle of cocoa powder, this potion is sure to enchant even the most wayward of witches.

Yield: *About 8 potion bottles* | **GF***

6 cups puffed rice cereal

10 ounces marshmallows

2 tablespoons salted butter, plus more for greasing marshmallow bowl and hands

1 to 2 drops light-blue food coloring

1 to 2 drops bright-green food coloring

1 cup marshmallow fluff

2 teaspoons black cocoa powder

1 cup sanding sugar

8 chocolate chew candies, unwrapped

Specialty Tools

Pastry bag

Note

This recipe can be easily made gluten-free by using gluten-free rice cereal.

Place the rice cereal in a large bowl. Grease a large microwave-safe bowl with butter and melt the marshmallows and 2 tablespoons butter in 30-second bursts. Stir until completely melted. Add the blue food coloring and stir until well incorporated.

Add the marshmallow mixture to the rice cereal and stir until completely combined.

In a small bowl, add the green food coloring to the marshmallow fluff, then transfer to a pastry bag. Set aside.

Add the cocoa powder to the cereal mixture and stir until incorporated. Do not overmix so you have a mottled coloring.

Place the sanding sugar on a shallow plate and have the chocolate chew candies standing by. Snip a small hole in the bottom of the pastry bag.

On a nonstick surface, such as parchment paper or a silicone baking mat, start to mold your "potion bottles." Grease your hands with a little butter and, using a 1-cup scoop of cereal mixture, mold it into a rough ball shape. Make a well in the middle and fill with about 1 tablespoon of marshmallow fluff. Close the cereal mixture over the marshmallow fluff and start building up to create the neck of the potion bottle. Keep compacting as you go but be careful not to squish out the marshmallow fluff. Use the parchment to flatten the base of the bottle so it will stand upright on its own.

To finish off your bottle, create a small hole in the top to place the chocolate chew candy (the "cork"). Press the cereal mixture around it.

Place the finished potion bottle bottom into the sanding sugar and push sugar up the sides about an inch or two to create the "potion." Repeat this process until all of the rice cereal mixture is gone, greasing your hands as necessary.

These can be stored in an airtight container for up to five days or in sealed cellophane bags to give as treats.

Desserts

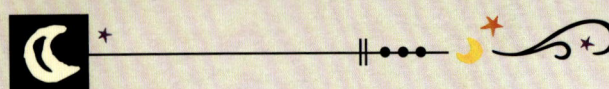

Tart Face Tart

Master's wife is *not* impressed when the tantalizing trio appears in her living room. Between Sarah's enchanting dance, Winifred's wicked sass, and Mary's overly familiar approach of making herself at home, the "little woman" quickly sours on her company. But it's her nickname for her unwanted guests that inspires this perfectly prickly treat. Berries fold neatly into a no-bake cookie crumb crust, making these tarts the ultimate dish to serve to company—invited or otherwise!

Yield: 8 servings | GF*, V

For the Filling
- 8 ounces cream cheese, softened
- ½ cup sugar
- 1 tablespoon sour cream
- 1 tablespoon fresh lime juice
- ½ cup heavy cream

For the Crust
- 1½ cups shortbread cookie crumbs (about 7 ounces of cookies, see note)
- Zest of 1 lime
- ¼ cup sugar
- 6 tablespoons salted butter, melted

For the Berry Topping
- 6 ounces golden or red raspberries
- Juice from 1 lime
- 2 tablespoons superfine sugar
- 4 ounces blueberries
- 4 ounces strawberries (optional)

Specialty Tools
- 9-inch tart pan

To make the filling: In a medium bowl using a hand mixer or in the bowl of a stand mixer fitted with the paddle attachment, cream together the cream cheese, sugar, sour cream, and lime juice on medium speed until light and fluffy, 1 to 2 minutes. Set aside. In another medium bowl, whip the cream on high speed until stiff peaks form and then fold it into the cream cheese mixture. Cover and refrigerate while making the crust.

To make the crust: Preheat the oven to 350°F.

In a medium bowl, mix together the cookie crumbs, lime zest, sugar, and melted butter. Pour the crumb mixture into a 9-inch tart pan and press it evenly on the bottom and up the sides.

Bake for 10 to 12 minutes, or until slightly golden. Remove from the oven and allow to cool completely on a wire rack. Baking the crust briefly makes for the easiest slicing, but for a truly no-bake version, freeze the crust for 15 or 20 minutes, until firm, before filling.

Once the tart shell is cool, spread the filling mixture into the pan and smooth it out evenly. Refrigerate for at least 2 hours or overnight.

continued on page 100

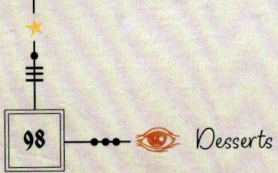

continued from page 98

To make the topping: When ready to serve, rinse the raspberries and place them on layered paper towels to dry completely. In a small bowl, mix together the lime juice and sugar, then set aside. Rinse the blueberries, drain thoroughly, and add them to the lime mixture, stirring to coat. Rinse, hull, and slice the strawberries (if using), then add them to the lime mixture, stirring to combine.

Arrange the raspberries along the top edge of the tart in two or three rows, creating "hair." Use a pastry brush to brush the berries with some of the juices from the bowl. Create eyes, blushing cheeks, and lips with some of the blueberries and strawberries. When serving, ladle extra berries and juice over each slice.

— *Notes* —

The cookies should be processed in a food processor until they are evenly crushed and sandy in texture. Measure out 1½ cups for the tart crust. You may have extra cookie crumbs.

This recipe can be easily made gluten-free by using your favorite gluten-free cookies in the crust.

Cat Tongue Cookies

When Thackery Binx goes missing, his father is beside himself. He demands that Winnie tell him what she's done, but Winnie slyly declares that the cat's got her tongue. These classic cookies offer a cheeky nod to Winnie's coy comment. Thin French cookie crisps with black tahini make this dessert so delicious, they won't stay a secret for long. Looks like the cat's out of the bag!

Yield: About 36 cookies | V

- 8 tablespoons (1 stick) unsalted butter
- 2 tablespoons black tahini
- 1 teaspoon vanilla extract
- ½ cup powdered sugar
- ¼ teaspoon ground cardamom
- 3 egg whites
- 1 large egg
- ¾ cup all-purpose flour

Specialty Tools
Pastry bag

> **Note**
> These cookies have a delicate flavor that pairs with your favorite cup of brew or Pumpkin Spiced Golden Milk (page 114).

Preheat the oven to 350°F. Line two baking sheets with parchment paper or silicone baking mats.

In a medium bowl with a hand mixer on medium-high speed, cream together the butter, tahini, and vanilla, until light and fluffy. Add the powdered sugar and cardamom and mix until incorporated. Slowly add the egg whites, mixing continually until completely incorporated, and then add the egg, mixing until the mixture is light and fluffy. Slowly add the flour, folding it in with a rubber spatula and scraping down the sides of the bowl as you go.

Load the batter into a pastry bag, then snip a ½-inch hole into the bottom. With the tip of the pastry bag raised off the surface of the baking sheet by approximately ¼ inch, pipe 2½- to 3-inch strips of batter spaced at least 3 inches apart. Repeat until both prepared baking sheets are full.

Bake, rotating halfway through if necessary, for 6 to 8 minutes, or until the edges are crisp and the centers are set. Allow to cool on the baking sheets before removing and storing in an airtight container for up to two days.

Frog Eggs Boba Matcha Cheesecake

Eye of newt and egg of frog . . .
Wait—no newt! That's for the glogg.
Substitute some cream cheese, then
Add in eggs, sugar (again),

Magic too—lest it be bland.
(Don't get banished from the land!)
With a swirl, you too shall make
A boba matcha cheesecake!

Yield: 1 cheesecake or 14 to 16 servings | GF*, V

For the Crust
- 2 cups (about 10 ounces) crushed ginger cookies
- 4 tablespoons unsalted butter, melted
- 3 tablespoons granulated sugar
- 1 tablespoon black cocoa powder

For the Cheesecake
- Four 8-ounce blocks cream cheese
- 2 tablespoons fresh lemon juice
- 1 tablespoon vanilla extract
- 1½ cups granulated sugar
- 5 large eggs

For the Matcha Topping
- 4 cups sour cream, divided
- ½ cup granulated sugar, divided
- 1 teaspoon vanilla extract
- 1½ tablespoons matcha

For the Boba and Syrup
- ½ cup granulated sugar
- ½ cup dark brown sugar
- 1 cup prepared brown sugar boba

Note: This recipe can be easily made gluten-free by using your favorite gluten-free cookies in the crust.

Preheat the oven to 350°F and have an 11-by-15-inch glass casserole pan standing by.

To make the crust: In the casserole pan, mix the crushed cookies, melted butter, sugar, and cocoa powder until well combined. Press the mixture until it evenly covers the bottom of the pan. Bake for 8 to 10 minutes, or until crisp and fragrant.

To make the cheesecake: While the crust bakes, combine the cream cheese, lemon juice, and vanilla in the bowl of a stand mixer fitted with the paddle attachment. Beat on medium speed until light and fluffy. Add the sugar and beat again until well combined. Add the eggs one at a time, beating to combine after each addition.

Pour the batter onto the crust and spread out evenly. Return the pan to the oven and bake for 30 to 40 minutes, or until the edges are puffed and the center is firm but wobbly.

To make the matcha topping: While the cheesecake bakes, have two medium bowls standing by. Divide the sour cream and sugar evenly between each bowl and stir to combine. Add the vanilla to one bowl and stir to combine. Add the matcha to the other bowl and stir to combine.

When the cheesecake base is done and out of the oven, use separate spoons to spoon generous dollops of each sour cream topping, alternating between the two flavors. Use a knife to swirl the two flavors together. Return the cheesecake to the oven and bake for 7 to 9 minutes more, or until the topping has set. Allow to cool completely on a wire rack, then cover and refrigerate until serving.

continued on page 104

continued from page 103

To make the boba syrup: In a small saucepan over medium-high heat, add 1 cup water, granulated sugar, and brown sugar. Bring to a boil, then turn the heat to medium-low and simmer for 1 minute. Remove from the heat and add the prepared boba pearls. Cover and allow to cool.

This syrup can be stored at room temperature for up to 4 hours or in the refrigerator overnight. Refrigerated boba pearls will have a firmer texture.

To serve, slice the chilled cheesecake into 3-by-3-inch squares and, using a slotted spoon, top with boba pearls.

Dust Bombs

Allison is well versed in the story of the Sandersons. While the black flame candle has brought the witches back to Salem for one night only, unless they can steal the life force of children, they'll be dust when the sun comes up. And when Winnie, Mary, and Sarah ultimately depart our earthly realm, they're destined to do so in a burst of glitter—a veritable dust bomb! This sparkling orb—concocted with edible glitter, sprinkles, and a handful of mini marshmallows—is perfect for breaking over ice cream . . . or any dessert that could benefit from just a touch of magic.

Yield: 3 bombs | GF

7 ounces dark chocolate melts

2 tablespoons purple sprinkles (see note)

1 teaspoon purple sparkle sugar

2 tablespoons red sprinkles

1 teaspoon red sparkle sugar

2 tablespoons green sprinkles

1 teaspoon green sparkle sugar

¼ cup mini marshmallows

Luster dust in purple, red, and green (optional)

Note

Have fun with the sprinkle sugar combos. The method is just a suggestion. Create a custom mix for each sister using their signature colors and even a tiny spider, rat, or bone. These are great to serve with two scoops of your favorite ice cream. Crack them open to "explode" sprinkles over the top.

Place one sphere mold on a baking sheet. In a medium microwave-safe bowl, melt the chocolate melts in 30-second bursts, stirring in between, for up to 90 seconds, until smooth.

Use a pastry brush to paint a thick layer of the melted chocolate into each mold. Be sure to go all the way up the side of the mold, to avoid any sheer spots. Refrigerate for 5 to 10 minutes, until set.

When the chocolate has set, carefully remove each half from the mold. (Don't worry if the edges chip a bit.)

Heat a microwave-safe plate (without anything on it) in the microwave for 30 to 45 seconds, until it's hot to the touch. Carefully remove the plate and cover it with a piece of parchment paper. Place half a sphere on the plate, rim-side down. Gently press and twist the sphere to clean up and flatten the edge. Place this half sphere back on the baking sheet and fill it with 2 tablespoons of purple sprinkles, 1 tablespoon of purple sparkle sugar, and 6 to 8 mini marshmallows.

Repeat the process with the second half sphere, again cleaning and heating up the edges. Gently press the two halves together, sealing in the sprinkles and marshmallows. Use melted chocolate from the plate to close any gaps.

Repeat this process with the remaining two sphere molds, chocolate, marshmallows, sprinkles, and sugar, using the different colors for each. Reheat the plate as necessary.

Dust each bomb with the coordinating luster dust (if using). Store in an airtight container for up to two weeks or package in cellophane bags for gift giving.

Drinks

Bubbling brews and creamy floats make up the final section of our witchy menu. From drinks inspired by each of the Sandersons—and beautifully reflecting their unique personalities—to the signature beverage of Salem's elite, the concoctions within these pages truly offer something for everyone. Most refreshing indeed!

Most Refreshing Drink

When Max summons the burning rain of death, the Sanderson sisters are quick to take cover. But this drink will have any witch—or even your average Salemite—crawling out of their grave to steal but a single sip. Lemon, lime, and a splash of the dreaded Burning Rain of Death syrup give this sparkling beverage its ghoulishly good flavor. And a meringue-made bone serves as a reminder of the fate that may befall those who cross the wrong witch . . . or her sisters!

Yield: 8 servings | GF, V, V+*

For the Meringue Bones
1 tablespoon meringue powder
1⅓ cups powdered sugar

For the Drink
1 cup fresh lime juice (about 12 limes)
1 cup fresh lemon juice (about 6 lemons)
½ cup syrup from Burning Rain of Death Drink (page 115), or more as desired
4 cups still or 1 cup sparkling water

Specialty Tools
Piping bag with medium writing tip

Note
This recipe can be easily made vegan if served without the meringue bones.

To make the meringue bones: In a small bowl using a hand mixer or the bowl of a stand mixer fitted with the whisk attachment, combine the meringue powder, powdered sugar, and 2 tablespoons water. Mix on high speed for 4 to 6 minutes. or until stiff peaks form.

Transfer the meringue mixture to a piping bag fitted with a medium writing tip and pipe out different bone shapes onto a piece of parchment paper. Allow to dry completely. Once the bones are dry, gently lift them from the parchment paper with an offset spatula. Store in an airtight container for up to two weeks until ready to serve.

To make the drink: Combine the lime and lemon juice, then strain them into an airtight container through a fine-mesh strainer, discarding the pulp. Combine the juices with the syrup and refrigerate until needed.

To serve, either combine all of the citrus mixture with the 4 cups of still water in a large pitcher with ice or combine ½ cup of the citrus mixture with 1 cup of the sparkling water over ice. Garnish each drink with a few meringue bones or place in a bowl next to the drink station.

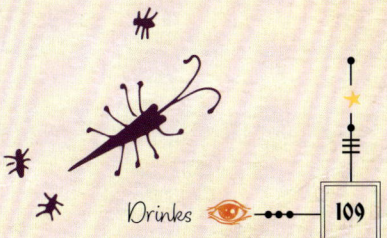

Drinks

"I Put a Spell on You" Brew

Max, Dani, and Allison sound the alarm at Salem's most populous Halloween party. The Sandersons have returned . . . and they're here to steal the lives of children! But when three dazzling women emerge from the crowd—each the spitting image of a Sanderson sister—they instantly *put a spell* on Salem's unwitting adults. And when these women burst into a toe-tapping, heart-pounding song-and-dance, the only thing that could snap the Salemites out of their trance is an *especially* strong brew. This one is a flavorful coffee beverage that certainly packs a punch . . . and it might just be the thing to lift the Sandersons' curse!

Yield: 2 servings | GF, V, V+*

2 cups cold coffee
2 tablespoons instant coffee
2 tablespoons sugar
½ cup half-and-half or preferred dairy

Specialty Tools
Ice cube trays
Milk frothing whisk

Note
This recipe can be easily made vegan by replacing the half-and-half with your favorite dairy substitute.

Pour the cold coffee into the ice cube trays and freeze overnight.

In a medium bowl or measuring cup, combine the instant coffee, sugar, and 2 tablespoons water. Whisk with a milk frother or by hand, about 2 minutes, until it forms a thick frosting-like consistency.

In another medium bowl or measuring cup, pour in the half-and-half and whisk with the milk frother or by hand until light and foamy, about 2 minutes.

Split the coffee ice cubes between two glasses, gently spoon the whipped half-and-half over the ice, and then top with half of the coffee foam.

Serve with spoons for stirring and enjoying.

Life Potion Witches' Drink

After capturing Emily Binx, Winnie brews a most devious potion before declaring, "One drop of this and her life will be mine!" With luscious green kiwi and bubbling ginger ale, this potion invokes the essence of Winnie's bewitching brew. (While omitting the less palatable ingredients of newt saliva and a bit of one's own tongue!) So enchanting is this brew, it's sure to have guests declaring, "Thou art divine!"

Yield: 6 servings | GF, V

- 4 ripe kiwis
- ½ cup pineapple juice
- ¼ teaspoon green luster dust
- 36 ounces ginger ale, chilled, divided

Note
Want to give your potion an extra kick? Use ginger beer instead of ginger ale.

Halve each kiwi and scoop out the flesh. Transfer it to the pitcher of a blender. Add the pineapple juice and blend until completely pureed. Strain the mixture through a fine-mesh strainer into a large measuring cup, pressing the mixture through. Discard the solids. Strain the mixture again, without pressing, to catch even more seeds.

Return the mixture to the blender, add the luster dust, and blend until completely incorporated. Refrigerate in an airtight container until ready to serve.

To serve, fill each of six glasses with ice, pour in about ¼ cup of the kiwi mixture, and top with about 6 ounces of chilled ginger ale. Gently stir and serve immediately.

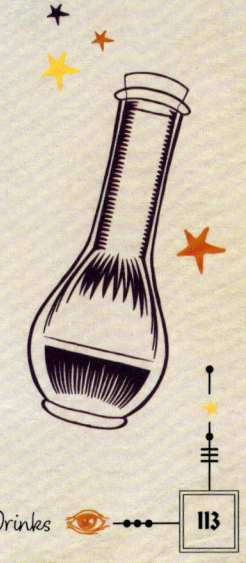

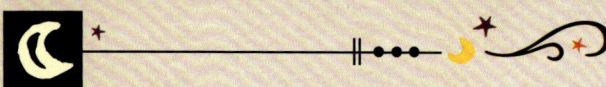

Pumpkin Spiced Golden Milk

Once he's to be Dani's cat,
Binx doth love where he is at.
He will have milk every day!
Prepared in the finest way.
For such spicy autumn brews,

Pumpkin's just the thing to use.
Blend it with some milk of gold
For a flavor that's quite bold.
Summon seasonings most sweet,
Stir lightly, and poof! A treat!

Yield: *2 servings* | GF, V, V+*

½ teaspoon fresh ground black pepper

1 teaspoon ground turmeric

2 cups unsweetened almond milk

3 tablespoons "No Witches Here" Pumpkin Butter (page 22) or store-bought pumpkin butter

1 to 2 tablespoons sweetener of choice, such as honey, agave, or maple syrup (optional)

In a medium heavy-bottomed saucepan set over medium heat, add the black pepper and turmeric. Stir with a wooden spoon and toast until fragrant, about 1 minute.

Add the almond milk, pumpkin butter, and sweetener (if using). Stir to combine and continue to cook until the pumpkin butter and sweetener have completely dissolved and the mixture is hot, 3 to 4 minutes. Decant into two heatproof mugs or glasses. Serve immediately.

Note
This recipe is vegan if using "No Witches Here" Pumpkin Butter, but if using store-bought, check the ingredients.

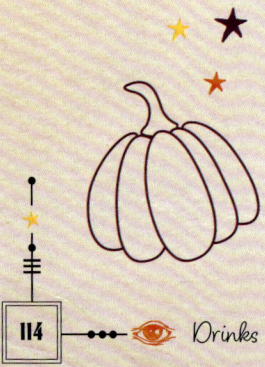

Burning Rain of Death Drink

With the Sanderson sisters reawakened, Max knows he has to flee their cottage . . . *fast*. Since the witches know nothing of indoor sprinklers, he's able to use this thoroughly modern tool to convince them that he's summoned the sinister, lethal *burning rain of death*. Luckily, there's nothing fearsome about its namesake drink. Winifred, Mary, and Sarah are respectively spicy, quirky, and sweet—just like this drink. With pink peppercorns, fresh ginger, and sugar, *this* Burning Rain of Death won't send one to one's demise. After all, 'tis but water . . . with a tantalizing twist!

> **Yield:** 1 cup of syrup, which can be used to flavor up to 12 cups of beverage | GF, V

1½ to 2 ounces fresh ginger, peeled and thinly sliced

1 cup sugar

1 teaspoon whole pink peppercorns

Sparkling water or cider for serving

Combine the ginger, sugar, and 1 cup water in a medium saucepan over medium-high heat and bring to a low boil, stirring often to dissolve the sugar. Turn the heat to medium-low and simmer for 15 minutes.

Remove from the heat, add the peppercorns, and allow to cool completely. Strain through a fine-mesh strainer into an airtight container and store in the refrigerator until ready to use or for up to ten days.

To serve, add 2 or 3 tablespoons of the syrup to a tall glass filled with ice and top with about 8 ounces of sparkling water.

Winnie's Popping Potion

Winifred Sanderson is many things—bold, saucy, and altogether unpredictable. It's only fitting that a drink bearing her name would combine all these characteristics . . . while adding an unexpected twist. This mocktail combines fresh tangy oranges with spicy Burning Rain of Death syrup (page 115) to create a blend that's both devilish and divine. With soothing mint and popping candy, Winnie's drink embraces the unexpected—just like Winnie herself!

Yield: 2 servings | GF, V, V+

2 or 3 oranges

About ¼ cup crushed Winnie's Magical Popping Candy (page 86)

2 lime quarters, divided

4 sprigs fresh mint, divided

1 cup fresh squeezed orange juice (about 2 oranges), divided

4 tablespoons syrup from Burning Rain of Death Drink (page 115)

About 16 ounces fizzy water

Peel wide strips of orange peel from the oranges, leaving the pith behind. Reserve the strips to create the twist garnishes. Juice the oranges. You need 1 cup of juice.

Place the popping candy on a plate or shallow dish. Rim two tall glasses with lime juice by running a lime quarter around the edge, then twist the rims in the popping candy so it sticks.

Add a lime quarter and two mint sprigs to each glass. Use a muddler or wooden spoon to muddle the mint and lime together. Fill each glass with ice. Add ½ cup of the orange juice and 2 tablespoons of the syrup to each glass.

Stir to combine. Top with fizzy water and garnish with the reserved orange twists.

Drinks

Sarah's Sassy Sipper

Sarah Sanderson skips to the beat of her own drum. As flighty as she is formidable, she uses her melodious voice to enchant the children of Salem . . . in hopes of sharing their very essence! It's only fitting that her mocktail embodies her sense of whimsy. With notes of hibiscus and a dollop of coconut milk, this drink is sure to take thee away, straight into a land of enchantment. 'Tis refreshing!

Yield: 4 servings | GF, V, V+

- 1 cup barista coconut milk
- 2 hibiscus berry tea bags
- 1 cup fresh or frozen blueberries
- ½ cup sugar
- 1 lemon
- 1 tablespoon sparkle sugar (optional)
- 16 ounces fizzy water, chilled, divided

In a small saucepan over medium-high heat, combine the coconut milk and hibiscus tea bags. Bring the mixture to a simmer, remove from the heat, and steep for 15 minutes. Remove the tea bags and refrigerate the flavored coconut milk in an airtight container until chilled and ready to serve.

In another small saucepan over medium-high heat, combine the blueberries, sugar, and ½ cup water. Bring to a boil, stirring and smashing the berries, and cook for 3 to 5 minutes. Remove from the heat and steep for 15 minutes. Strain through a fine-mesh strainer into an airtight container and discard the solids. Cover and refrigerate until chilled and ready to serve.

To serve, quarter the lemon and run each quarter around the rim of each of four glasses, reserving the lemon quarters for garnish. Place the sparkle sugar (if using) on a rimmed plate and twist each glass rim in the sugar so it sticks. Fill each glass with ice, pour ¼ cup of the blueberry syrup into each glass, and top with ¼ cup of the coconut mixture. Top off each glass with about 4 ounces of fizzy water, garnish with a wedge of lemon, and serve.

Mary's Magic Elixir

Mary Sanderson is the peacekeeper of the family. When things get stressful, she's the first to suggest a calming circle. And she gently reminds her fierier sister of the importance of being honest with thyself. Her frothy mocktail is as grounded as its namesake, with earthy notes of cherry, a subtle thread of cocoa, and a dollop of cranberry syrup drizzled atop cocoa-flavored whipped cream—a fitting tribute to the crimson streak that graces Mary's hair. After just a few sips, you'll be sure to declare, "I *am* calm!"

Yield: 2 servings | GF, V

½ cup pure unsweetened cranberry juice

¼ cup cranberry syrup from Popping Cranberries (page 27)

½ cup heavy cream

1 tablespoon chocolate syrup

16 ounces fizzy water, divided

6 Popping Cranberries (page 27)

Specialty Tools
Pastry bag and large star tip

In a 1-cup measuring cup, mix together the cranberry juice and syrup. In a medium bowl using a hand mixer on high speed, whip together the heavy cream and chocolate syrup until stiff peaks form.

Fill two tall glasses with ice and split the cranberry mixture between them. Fill each glass with about 8 ounces of the fizzy water. Use a pastry bag fitted with a large star tip or a spoon to pile the chocolate whipped cream on top of each drink. Garnish with the cranberries and serve immediately.

Drinks

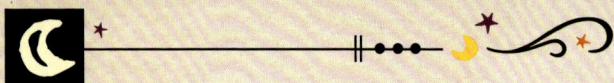

Sunrise Punch

Salem's infamous, witchy trio has only until sunrise to enact their sinister spell. If they can usurp the youth from the town's children, immortality will be theirs! But if Winifred, Mary, and Sarah can't break their curse before the dawn, they'll be in for a real *punch*. Just like the Sandersons' hour of reckoning, this tasty, tropical brew evokes notes of a bright new day. It's just the thing to usher in another glorious morning—whether as youthful, attractive witches . . . or mere specks of dust!

Yield: *8 servings* | GF, V, V+

One 10-ounce bag frozen cherries

1 orange, sliced

½ grapefruit, sliced

1 cup cherry juice

1 cup grapefruit juice

2 cups orange juice

In a large pitcher, layer the cherries, sliced oranges, and sliced grapefruit. Pour in the cherry juice.

Fill the pitcher with ice and then add the grapefruit juice, followed by the orange juice. Serve immediately. Provide tongs to serve fruit with each glass.

--- Note ---

Having a party? Double the recipe. Set up two pitchers with fruit in each and keep one pitcher in the freezer. When the second pitcher is needed, add the juice and ice as above.

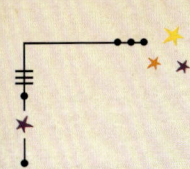

Conclusion

Curses! The dawn nears, and our time together must draw to a close. Hopefully, these alimentary offerings have brought a ghostly glimmer—and perhaps a sprinkle of magic—to your table. After all, 'tis not every day that one can summon a menu with such a distinguished trio in mind. Whether your tastes run toward the spicy—in which case, we do hope you sampled The Master's Fried Peppers—or the sweet—perhaps the sinfully sinister Cat Tongue Cookies were more to your liking—we fervently hope that your appetite has been fully sated. But should you find yourself with an insatiable hunger, by all means light the black flame candle and start your adventure anew. The Sanderson sisters would certainly understand!

We're devilishly delighted that you've joined us on our culinary carousing. After such a fine feast, you're no doubt ready for a good, long rest—just like the ever-mindful Sanderson sister who once loudly declared, "I *am* calm!" It is our deepest desire that you come back to these pages again and again. After all, there is much magic to be found within books—whether that tome is bound in human skin or mere paper. We do hope these recipes have *put a spell on you*. As Winifred says, "Life is sweet—be not shy." Now, on thy feet—so sayeth I!

Glossary

BLIND BAKING: Blind baking means baking pastry or crumb crust without any filling. This method is used when the filling will not be baked at all, such as with a whipped cream or pudding, when the filling needs less time than the crust to bake, or when the filling is quite wet, such as pumpkin pie, and you want to protect the crust from sogginess.

BLUE SPIRULINA: Blue spirulina is extracted from a blue-green algae that grows in ponds, lakes, and alkaline waterways. It is rich in vitamins, antioxidants, and proteins, providing a deep blue color when used in recipes. It is available online and in most health food stores.

BUTTERFLY PEA FLOWERS: Butterfly pea flowers are commonly used in herbal tea drinks. When added to a recipe, they provide a beautiful deep blue color. If combined with acids, like lemon juice, the color shifts to pink or purple. They are available online and in some health food stores.

CANDY THERMOMETER: Candy thermometers, sometimes called fry thermometers, are long thermometers that can be clipped to the side of your pot and withstand very high temperatures of at least 500°F. They are used to measure temperatures of frying oil or sugar during the creation of syrups, candies, and certain frostings.

CHOCOLATE MELTING POT: A plug-in device with a removable silicone pot that melts chocolate and then keeps it warm and at the correct temperature for dipping and coating things like cake pops or berries.

CUTTING IN BUTTER: To work cold butter into dry ingredients until it is broken down into small pea-size pieces and dispersed evenly throughout the mixture. It is important that the butter is very cold so it does not begin to soften. These little pieces of butter surrounded by the dry ingredient are what create the flakiness in pastry.

DEGLAZE: Deglazing is adding liquid, usually wine or stock, to a hot pan to release all of the caramelized food from the pan. These caramelized bits, called fond, are full of flavor and should not be left behind. Deglazing is often the first step in making a delicious sauce.

DUTCH OVEN: A Dutch oven is a heavy cooking pot often made out of cast iron that is ideal for making stews or deep-frying because it will hold and distribute heat evenly. It works well with high or low temperatures and is a versatile cooking tool that is a handy addition to every kitchen.

EGG WASH: Whisk together an egg and 1 tablespoon of water until light and foamy. Use a pastry brush to apply when the recipe requires.

FOLDING IN: This refers to gently adding an ingredient with a spatula in wide gentle strokes. Do not whisk or stir vigorously. Folding allows any airiness already established to stay intact.

LUSTER DUST: A food-safe glitter that can be purchased online or in specialty baking departments. It can be mixed with clear alcohol to create a shimmery paint or brushed on dry.

MACERATE: Macerating is similar to marinating but for fruit. Combining the fruit with a little bit of liquid, such as citrus or vinegar, and often a bit of sugar, allows the fruit to soften and release some of its juices, resulting in a delicious syrup.

MILK: The word milk in this book is always referring to dairy milk unless otherwise noted. In most cases, any percentage of milk fat will do unless otherwise noted.

PARSLEY: When parsley is used as an ingredient in this book, please use flat-leaf parsley, as opposed to curly parsley.

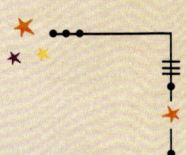

PEELING GINGER: The easiest way to peel fresh ginger is with a small spoon. Simply use the edge of the spoon to scrape away the peel. This keeps the ginger root intact, with less waste, and allows you to easily navigate all the bumps and lumps.

RENDERING FAT: The term "rendering fat" used in this book refers to cooking off the fat of the piece(s) of meat. The fat should melt into the pan while the meat left behind becomes brown and crispy.

SALT: Feel free to use your salt of choice unless it has been noted in the recipe. Kosher salt is the one most commonly used throughout the book.

SHIMMERING OIL: Shimmering oil is hot but not to smoke point. You know it's "shimmering" when it spreads out quickly across the pan, has a rippled look across the surface, and glistens.

SILICONE BAKING MAT: Silicone baking mats can withstand high temperatures in the oven and low temperatures in the freezer. They are very helpful in baking because they are easy to roll dough out on and can then go from prep station to chilling to oven without having to move dough. They are extremely nonstick and easy to clean.

SPIDER: A spider is a long-handled spoon with a fine-mesh basket in the shape of a shallow bowl. Traditionally, the mesh is hand-tied with wide lattice-like openings, and the long handle keeps your hands away from pesky things, like bubbling hot oil. Its unusual name comes from the spider-web pattern created by the wire.

SUMAC: Made from ground berries of the sumac flower, this sour, acidic spice is most commonly used in Mediterranean and Middle Eastern cooking. It is particularly popular in dry rubs, marinades, and dressings. Try sprinkling some over your food just before serving for extra flavor and a punch of color. If you are unable to find sumac at your local grocer, you can use lemon zest, but use less than the called-for amount of sumac as the lemon zest has a more potent flavor.

INSIGHT EDITIONS
PO Box 3088
San Rafael, CA 94912
www.insighteditions.com

Find us on Facebook: www.facebook.com/InsightEditions
Follow us on Twitter: @insighteditions

Copyright © 2023 Disney

All rights reserved. Published by Insight Editions, San Rafael, California, in 2023.

No part of this book may be reproduced in any form without written permission from the publisher.

Gift ISBN: 979-8-88663-278-1

Publisher: Raoul Goff
VP, Co-Publisher: Vanessa Lopez
VP, Creative: Chrissy Kwasnik
VP, Manufacturing: Alix Nicholaeff
VP, Group Managing Editor: Vicki Jaeger
Publishing Director: Jamie Thompson
Designer: Leah Bloise Lauer
Editor: Anna Wostenberg
Editorial Assistant: Emma Merwin
Managing Editor: Maria Spano
Senior Production Editor: Michael Hylton
Production Associate: Deena Hashem
Senior Production Manager, Subsidiary Rights: Lina s Palma-Temena

Photographer: Ted Thomas
Assistant Photographer: Jason Rogers
Food and Prop Stylist: Elena P. Craig
Assistant Food Stylist: August Craig
Decorator and Assistant Food Stylist: Patricia Parrish
Photoshoot Art Direction: Judy Wiatrek Trum

Special thanks to Rusty Hinges Ranch for use of their space for photography.

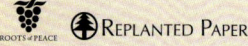

Insight Editions, in association with Roots of Peace, will plant two trees for each tree used in the manufacturing of this book. Roots of Peace is an internationally renowned humanitarian organization dedicated to eradicating land mines worldwide and converting war-torn lands into productive farms and wildlife habitats. Roots of Peace will plant two million fruit and nut trees in Afghanistan and provide farmers there with the skills and support necessary for sustainable land use.

Manufactured in China by Insight Editions

10 9 8 7 6 5 4 3 2 1